Introduction to Hegel's *Philosophy of History*

Introduction to Hegel's
Philosophy of History

Jean Hyppolite

Translated by Bond Harris and
Jacqueline Bouchard Spurlock

With a Foreword by Arkady Plotnitsky

University Press of Florida
Gainesville/Tallahassee/Tampa/Boca Raton
Pensacola/Orlando/Miami/Jacksonville

Jean Hyppolite, *Introduction à la philosophie de l'histoire de Hegel*, first published 1948, 1968 reimpression, Editions Marcel Rivière et Cie, Paris. Copyright 1983 by Editions du Seuil, Paris.

01 00 99 98 97 96 6 5 4 3 2 1

Library of Congress Cataloging-in-Publication Data

Hyppolite, Jean.
    [Introduction à la philosophie de l'histoire de Hegel. English]
    Introduction to Hegel's philosophy of history / by Jean Hyppolite; translated by Bond Harris and Jacqueline Spurlock; with a foreword by Arkady Plotnitsky.
    p. cm.
    Includes bibliographical references and index.
    ISBN 0-8130-1458-1 (alk. paper)
    1. Hegel, Georg Wilhelm Friedrich, 1770–1831—Contributions in philosophy of history. 2. History—Philosophy. I. Title.
D16.8.H913   1996   96-32322
901—dc20

The University Press of Florida is the scholarly publishing agency for the State University System of Florida, comprised of Florida A & M University, Florida Atlantic University, Florida International University, Florida State University, University of Central Florida, University of Florida, University of North Florida, University of South Florida, and University of West Florida.

University Press of Florida
15 Northwest 15th Street
Gainesville, FL 32611

Contents

Foreword

Reading and Rereading Hyppolite and Hegel

Arkady Plotnitsky

> Pour nous Français, la vision du monde de Hegel . . . est
> indispensable à connaître.
> *Hyppolite*
> Die Weltgeschichte ist das Weltgericht.
> *Hegel/Schiller*

This foreword is an invitation to read and to reread both Hyppolite and Hegel. My aim is to suggest what may be at stake in reading Jean Hyppolite's book (first published in 1948) or encountering or reencountering Hyppolite's monumental encounter with Hegel at the close of this—the most Hegelian and the most anti-Hegelian—century.

Both Hyppolite's project in the introduction and his encounter with Hegel as a whole are defined by bringing together four dimensions of modern philosophy and the political world—history, politics, materiality, and tragedy—with history providing the main axis to Hyppolite's vision. One would expect Marx to appear first in this context, and he was indeed a figure of paramount significance for Hyppolite. Nietzsche, however, is no less (perhaps more) significant here, especially once tragedy enters the scene, for Hyppolite and for most other major French figures whose thought was shaped by their encounters with Hegel's philosophy. The list of these figures is long, and they represent the extraordinary richness of the intellectual and cultural life of twentieth-century France and define our contemporary—modern or postmodern—intellectual landscape.

As a major thinker, a great scholar, a translator of Hegel, a professor at and a director of the Ecole Normale (1954–1963), and finally a professor at the Collège de France, Hyppolite was a major shaping force of this landscape.[1] Foucault said, "A large part of [my] indebtedness . . . is to Jean Hyppolite."[2] Both Deleuze and Derrida owe debts to Hyppolite as well, and Deleuze's first book, *Empiricisme et subjectivité,* was dedicated to Hyppolite.[3]

Heidegger argued that a meaningful encounter with Hegel entails the necessity to "go along with Hegel at length and with patience, that is, with labor."[4] It is difficult to think of a better example here than Hyppolite, whose experience of Hegel is the experience of this pressing necessity of reading and rereading Hegel. This necessity is a heavy burden, for paradoxically, the difficulty of Hegel multiplies with an increase in rigor and comprehensiveness of reading. The increase in knowledge of Hegel opens and enlarges spaces of a new—as yet unknown—Hegel and, with Hegel, of intellectual inquiry. This double economy defines our understanding of Hegel, from Feuerbach and Marx on, and is central to Hyppolite's reading and his view of Hegel and of the history of philosophy. It both partly mirrors—*reflects*—and partly operates against Hegel's philosophy and his concepts of knowledge and reflection and of the development and unfolding of knowledge. It also reflects Hegel's view of his own philosophical enterprise as what Nietzsche calls philosophy of the future and his view of himself as a philosopher of the future.[5] Philosophy of the future, however, would not be possible without creating new spaces of the unknown and ultimately the unknowable (along with an increase in knowledge) and without offering a possibility to continue this joint process into the future. "Knowledge is the access to the unknown," and finally the unknowable— Bataille says.[6] He offers this great insight (in part) against Hegel and his concept of absolute knowledge in his own momentous confrontation with Hegel. The statement, however, is not an impossible, and perhaps even the best, interpretation of Hegel's philosophy and of absolute knowledge. It is also in accord with Hyppolite's vision of Hegel and his role in the history of philosophy. Hyppolite's encounter with Hegel is itself an extraordinary example of expanding both knowledge and the unknown, and entering the threshold of the unknowable, which may be the only sense of progress in our understanding of Hegel, or of progress of knowledge in general, still available to us. Nietzsche writes in *The Birth of Tragedy*:

> [S]cience, spurred by its powerful delusion, speeds irresistibly toward its limit where its optimism, concealed in the essence of logic, suffers shipwreck. For the periphery of science has an infinite number of points; and while there is no telling how this circle can ever be surveyed completely, noble and gifted men nevertheless reach, e'er half of their time and inevitably, such boundary points on the periphery from which one gazes into what defies illumination. When they see to their horror how logic coils up at these boundaries and finally

bites its own tail—suddenly the new form of insight breaks through, *tragic insight* which, merely to be endured needs art as a salvation and remedy.[7]

This passage may even be an implicit commentary on Hegel's conclusion of the *Phenomenology*, Hegel's own tremendous confrontation with the unknowable, his own boundary point, which he reached, e'er half of his time and inevitably, and from which he gazed into what defies illumination, as did Dante and Nietzsche himself. (Nietzsche explicitly alludes here to the opening line of Dante's *Divine Comedy*.) Nietzsche also alludes to Hegel's analysis of art toward the end of the book and to Hegel's *Aesthetics*, which famously announced "the death of art" and which can be read in the same way. Both Nietzsche's original title of the book "the *re*birth of tragedy out of the spirit of music," and his own, equally famous, pronouncement, twice repeated in *The Birth of Tragedy* (52, 141), "only as an *aesthetics phenomenon* that existence and the world are eternally *justified*," too, appear to allude to Hegel's concept of "the death of art" and another of his famous maxims, "die Weltgeschichte ist das Weltgericht" [history of the world is the judgment of the world] (a quotation from Schiller's 1794 poem "Resignation").[8] This understanding of history and the statement itself are crucial to Hyppolite, specifically in this study, where he argues that this insight, too, must be seen as a tragic insight—the insight into the tragedy of the world, and the tragic nature of history and of judgment.

In this book, written in 1948, Hyppolite argues that Hegel's philosophy is indispensable, especially "for us French," and he reiterated and nuanced this claim throughout his writing. In 1966, in closing "The Structure of Philosophical Language," he offers his final statement on Hegel: Hegel "well knew, in the words of my friend Merleau-Ponty, that there is no philosopher without a shadow."[9] Earlier in the essay Hyppolite says that Hegel's "great shadow falls over all the philosophical essays which have been written either for or against him" (158), or those that try to ignore or to turn away from him, such as Deleuze, that great student of Leibniz and Spinoza, but also of Hyppolite and, against himself, of Hegel.[10] One is well warned by Heidegger, Bataille, Derrida, and, of course, Hyppolite that Hegelianism extends its power even when ignored, turned away from, and the Hegelianism emerging as a result is often of the worst type. Hegel makes it impossible for one to treat him lightly, even when one refuses to treat him, and he makes it difficult to break from him, in part because his philosophy is a philosophy of both continuity and break, including break from itself, or from all philosophy. Instead one must oscillate between the possibilities (or necessities) and impossibilities of reading, radical but never absolute departures from and radical but never absolute continuities with Hegel and classical philosophy. The proximities and differences, continuities and breaks, departures and impossibilities of departure (or returns) are never fully decidable or determinable, and sometimes pass into each other. Hyppolite's encounter with Hegel continuously reflects on this economy, and as such becomes the scene of a great experiment for Hyppolite himself and for his students and readers—the scene of a philosophy of the future. As Foucault writes, "For Hyppolite, the relationship [with Hegel] was the scene of an experiment, of a confrontation in which it was never certain that philosophy would come out on top. He never saw the Hegelian system as a reassuring universe; he saw in it the field in which philosophy took the ultimate risk" (*Archeology of Knowledge*, 235–36).

The question of what is still possible or impossible for philosophy has been one of the central questions not only of modern intellectual history but also of the history of philosophy, which from its unknown *birth* (if this concept can apply) has been shaped by the question of the end or the *death* of philosophy. It would be difficult to argue that Hegel ever unequivocally speaks of the end of either history or philosophy, or indeed of art. At issue instead are transformations and new forms of inquiry and practice. Nor would this point be contradicted by Hegel's famous "owl of Minerva" passage on the belatedness of philosophy in *The Philosophy of Right*: "When philosophy paints its grey in grey, a shape of life has grown old, and it cannot be rejuvenated, but only recognized, by the grey in grey of philosophy; the owl of Minerva begins its flight only with the onset of the dusk" (*The Philosophy of Right*, 23). For this statement, too, may be read as suggesting that philosophy must always be—and that true philosophy can only be—philosophy of the future, a philosophy for new stages of life and spirit. At the end of the *Phenomenology* Hegel presents the perpetual unfolding and renewal of spirituality and philosophy through the image of the Phoenix, rather than of the owl of Minerva: "[A]bsorbed in itself, [Spirit] is sunk in the night of self-consciousness; but in that night its vanished outer existence is preserved, and this transformed existence—the former one, but now reborn of the Spirit's knowledge—is the new existence, a new world and a new shape of Spirit."[11]

"Isn't it too late to focus our attention on Hegel? What can we learn from him? What have we to ask him?" Hyppolite asks in 1966 ("The Structure of Philosophical Language," 158). It appears that it is always a bit too late, and yet never too early to ask these questions again in this seemingly eternal recurrence of Hegel. Since 1966 we have witnessed several returns of these questions and transformations of Hegel—from structuralism to poststructuralism and postmodernism to recent preoccupations with the political and ideological concerns of the 1980s and 1990s. Most recently Hegel has returned in the debate about the end of history in the wake of the geopolitical transformations that created post-Soviet Europe. Hegel's philosophy, which is also the philosophy of such processes themselves, may remain *a* philosophy—if not *the* philosophy—of the future for a while.

There are thus many reasons to read and some reasons to avoid reading Hegel; and it may not be impossible to claim with certainty either to have read or to have avoided reading him. That said, however, one might still ask: Why read Hyppolite? Why read Hyppolite now, especially his 1948 work, rather than other major encounters with Hegel, more prominent in recent years and reflecting more recent philosophical and political developments?

There are several reasons that might be offered here—beyond the significance of Hyppolite's interpretation of Hegel and Hegelianism. They include Hyppolite's emphases on the fundamentally historical character of Hegel's philosophy, on a codetermination of history and politics in Hegel, and on the question of materiality in Hegel's "idealist" philosophy. All these issues have major contemporary resonances, and I shall comment on them presently. History, however, remains a crucial reason for reading his work and perhaps can never be left aside. How can historical considerations be left aside while and after reading Hegel or Hyppolite? Both fundamentally connect reason, or philosophy, and history, including in the context of philosophical education, such as Hegel's or Hyppolite's own. The continuing historical processing of Hegel is also the process of *understanding* Hegel's philosophy and what is at stake in it. But then, as Hegel taught us, his philosophy itself emerges in these transformations, which also produce certain, more or less stable, configurations of questions (or answers) or readings, and certain, more or less stable, (past) histories. The debates, even daily debates, around Hegel are among the most extraordinary debates in modern intellectual history, to which Hyppolite's work was one of the most extraordinary contributions, and they have been and remain a crucial part of our own philosophical and political debate.

The political stakes of these debates are equally significant—from the politics of philosophy and its institutions to geopolitics—as again in recent discussions of the end, or many ends (in either sense, "goal" and "termination") of history.[12] In 1968 in the last article he wrote before his death, Hyppolite remarked that "the current state of our planet leads to new questions about Marxism, to a return to the works and fundamental texts of Marx, which cannot be separated from Lenin's interpretation."[13] This last claim was open to challenge even then, let alone now, when this history is perhaps (a very big perhaps) at its end or some of its ends. The very possibility of challenge is important for it is also through challenges, philosophical or political, that we learn Hegel's philosophy.

Both Hegel and Hyppolite tell us that history can never be left behind. Moreover, and this is one of Hyppolite's central points, this history is also conceived as actual material history rather than in terms of an abstract, and especially an ahistorical, concept of history, even though and because a crucial part of Hegel's understanding of history is that (a "concept" of) history as free of concepts—or of philosophy—is itself an ahistorical abstraction. He undertook a radical critique of both an uncritical (which is also ahistorical) formalism and an uncritical (which is also aphilosophical) historicism. His concept of history or, conversely, philosophy and what he calls *the* Concept is defined by joining history and conceptuality. He closes the *Phenomenology* at this juncture, fulfilled in what he calls the conceptually comprehended History: "The two together, the conceptually comprehended History, form alike the interiorization and the Calvary of Absolute Spirit, the actuality, truth, and certainty of his throne, without which he would be lifeless and alone" (493, translation modified).

In concluding his elaboration on the limits of logic, cited earlier, Nietzsche writes in *The Birth of Tragedy:*

> Concerned but not disconsolate, we stand aside a little while, contemplative men to whom it has been granted to be witnesses of these tremendous struggles and transitions. Alas, it is the magic of these struggles that those who behold them must also take part and fight. (98)

Hegel is one of the greatest participants in—and one of the greatest philosophers of—"these tremendous struggles and transitions," and he must have been on Nietzsche's mind here. Nietzsche retains the Hegelian significance of history, or proceeds from the (counter-Hegelian) rebirth or resurrection of art to history and toward Hegel—or both toward and against Hegel. Even more significant here are elaborations on art and the Dionysian toward the end of the *Phenomenology,* where Hegel makes his arguably most Nietzschean pronouncement, "God is dead," to which Hyppolite refers at an equally Nietzschean point of *Genesis and Structure* (557). In closing his discussion, Hyppolite invokes, first, "human all too human" (which is the title of the first book of Nietzsche's mature period) and then "the death of God":

> "Self is absolute essence," but this self must discover its inconsistency; when it claims to attain itself, it finds itself alienated from itself. By itself finite, *it is human, all too human* [Hyppolite's emphasis]. The truth of this absolute self-certainty is that it is the opposite of itself; it claims to be happy consciousness, but it must learn that it is unhappy consciousness, the consciousness for which "God himself is dead." Thus it is the arena for a higher form of religion, Christianity. But in this dialectic of Greek comedy, we find a thought which continuously reappears in Hegelianism: man is the truth of the divine, but each time that he reduces the divine to himself, each time he loses the movement of transcending himself, he loses himself. Hence the harsh phrase: "God himself is dead." (557)

The idea of the Dionysian is pivotal for the *Phenomenology,* which makes the book Nietzschean or makes some of Nietzsche's ideas Hegelian. Thus Hegel writes:

> The True is the Bacchanalian revel in which no member is not drunk; yet because each member dissolves as soon as he separates, the revel is just as much transparent and simple repose. Judged in the court of this movement, the single shapes of Spirit do not persist any more than determinate thoughts do, but they are as much positive and necessary moments as they are negative and evanescent. (27–28, translation modified)

The contours of an artistic—Dionysian and Nietzschean—philosophy of the future emerge here—a more Nietzschean Hegel, a more Hegelian Nietzsche. One of the products of this philosophy is one of the greatest insights, on both Hegel's and Nietzsche's part, in the history of Western thought—*the birth of tragedy is the death of God*—which also establishes an overarching theme of all Nietzsche's Dionysian philosophy, from the earliest to the latest. We have as yet barely explored the meaning and implications, philosophical and political, of this idea, even those of us who claim

merely or instead that God does not exist. The latter idea is far less profound, and certainly less tragic in either sense. The idea of the death of God
acquires an even more profound meaning in view of its birth out of—or its
giving birth to—the spirit of tragedy. Thus, their revolutionary aspirations
notwithstanding, most forms of Marxism and related developments remain complicit with the idealist systems that they try to overthrow, or are
not radical enough to do so. Along with idealism, such materialism, too,
remains, as Nietzsche writes, "human, all too human": "Idealism, for example; the title means: 'where *you* see ideal things, *I* see what is'—human,
alas, all-too-human!"[14]

Although, beyond Hegel himself, Marx appears to be the central shaping force of the present book, Nietzsche must have been on Hyppolite's
mind at its key junctures, especially in the connections between history,
politics, and tragedy which define Hyppolite's analysis. For, according to
Hyppolite, "the notion of the [historical] spirit of the people and the tragic
vision of the world" are "in the center of Hegelian thought" (*Introduction*,
124). While the subject of the book is Hegel's earlier works, it is clear that
Hyppolite's thinking is fundamentally shaped by the conjunction of tragedy, materiality, history, and politics that emerges toward the end of the
Phenomenology. This conjunction played a major role in subsequent intellectual history, if often without recognition of its Hegelian origin or the
degree to which the "idealist" Hegel already explored its materialist dimensions, whether one speaks of physical or historico-political materiality.

This understanding may well be the greatest contribution of this book.
First of all, while Hyppolite's *Introduction* is to Hegel's philosophy of
history, it is also and perhaps primarily on politics and on the materialism
of politics. He argues that the historico-political economy was Hegel's
major concern since his earliest works, and his philosophy of history is that
of history as politics, which also means material political economy (in
either sense, given the significance of Adam Smith for Hegel, often stressed
by Hyppolite). Hence, secondly, the profound connections among history,
politics, and materiality in Hegel—the greatest idealist philosopher—and
as in Nietzsche's case, Hegel's tragic sense of life and the tragic nature of
his vision enhance rather than diminish the role of materiality in his philosophy.

There are several points in this book where the question of the "materialist" Hegel emerges. Perhaps most profoundly, however, it is posed in
Hyppolite's closing elaborations. First he points out that "in Hegel's final
philosophy, which desires to comprehend the reconciliation which religion

only senses, one is thus led to wonder what are the relations of objective spirit and absolute spirit, the latter appearing to itself in various forms of the world of art, religion and philosophical thought" (*Introduction,* 124). While Hyppolite might refer primarily to such works as the first *Logic,* the *Encyclopedia,* and the *Philosophy or Right,* this question, as he also points out, emerges earlier: "In the course of 1805–1806 and later in the *Phenomenology* of 1807 religion is not only religion of a people: it is consciousness of the absolute distinct from the objective development of the idea in history" (124). Hyppolite is referring to actual human history as the objective form of Spirit's existence in the world. As Hegel writes in the *Phenomenology:* "The movement of carrying forward the form of [Spirit's] self-knowledge is the labor which it accomplishes as actual History" (488). This self-knowledge, however, is also conceived by Hegel as *exceeding* actual history. This excess leads to crucial questions and complications with which Hyppolite closes or uncloses his study:

> But this question poses the problem of the interpretation of the complete Hegelian system. It is fundamental to determine in the final analysis the meaning of this system. However, this goes beyond our task, and moreover, it is uncertain that our philosopher always presents a perfectly clear solution. There exists in his thought an ambiguity. That ambiguity is that the reconciliation of subjective spirit and objective spirit, the supreme synthesis of this system, is perhaps not completely realizable. (124–25)

This ambiguity remains unresolved, both in Hegel and, in relation to Hegel's (un)resolution, in Hyppolite. Hyppolite formulates this question here (in 1948) in the classical terms of objective and subjective spirit. The economy of ambiguity and (un)resolution themselves emerging here may, however, no longer be classical and may require other terms. Such questions arise most dramatically when Hegel closes his major works; and Hyppolite's unclosing gesture here repeats Hegel's.

Hegel's elaboration is parallel to and is perhaps a source of Nietzsche's elaboration on the limits of logic, which analogously approaches the closure of the first version of *The Birth of Tragedy.* Both Hegel and Nietzsche move from the limits of logic and science to history, which they both witness and in which, by doing so, they must take part. Such, we recall, is the magic of these struggles and transitions—and of these books.

Hegel's concept of sacrifice implies the necessity of a radical revision of all metaphysical materiality—that is, materiality conceived uncritically, for example, as reality existing (absolutely) independently of its inscription. It is true that the conclusion of the *Phenomenology* may and, to a degree, must be read and critically scrutinized or deconstructed as one of the highest points of philosophical idealism and of the idealist unity of science and history, indeed as the culmination and the closure—and (en)closure—of European idealism. Even in this reading Hegel's text would retain an extraordinary critical potential, for example, for a deconstruction of uncritically materialist philosophies of nature or history. The ambiguity of Hegel's thought invoked by Hyppolite suggests, however, the possibility of a more radical—more materialist or more reciprocal or interactive— reading. This possibility is, I think, more significant, at least at this point of history. The force of this reading consists in the new possibilities that it offers for the very concept of "materiality" and for a more interactive or reciprocal (in relation to, for example, phenomenology) conceptuality of matter and material history, politics, and culture. Hegel proceeds here in part against Kant, although Kant's ideas may entail an equally ambivalent inscription of materiality. Whatever the case may be in Kant, Hegel's analysis suggests that matter can no longer be conceived unproblematically as a thing-in-itself, as existing in itself and by itself independently of its inscription, conceptuality, history, culture, politics, and so forth. Nor, conversely, can its radical (but, it follows, never absolute) alterity be fully contained by any given inscription.

This point can be and, in various degrees, has been made (by Nietzsche, Bataille, Lacan, Derrida, and others) more directly, proceeding against such forms of metaphysics of matter, for example, in Marxist materialism as a metaphysics or, one might say, idealism of matter, as in Lenin's famous definition of matter as an objective reality existing independently of consciousness. Hegel's inscription and its irreducible ambivalence, however, appear to offer richer possibilities in this respect. While I cannot consider in detail the conceptuality that emerges as a result and its implications (one more reason to read Hegel and Hyppolite), two main (clusters of) points can be made here.

First, Hegel tells us that matter (even in physics, let alone the materiality of history) requires all the complexity—and, one might add, all the ambiguity—of spirit. This is a great lesson of nineteenth- and twentieth-century science, and the point was made by great materialist thinkers such as Marx and Nietzsche. This point implies that we need complex or global economies in order to describe what are traditionally seen as simple or local economies; we need economies of the whole in order to describe the parts. Thus, to use an example especially pertinent for this book, we need to model memory or biography on history, global history—perhaps even world history—rather than, as has often been done, including on occasion by Hegel himself, the other way around (that is, seeing history as a kind of memory or biography). Against the order of classical logic, the complex appears always to precede the simple.

Second, what becomes necessary is irreducible reciprocity or interactiveness between spirit or mind and matter, between ideality (or phenomenality) and materiality, and so forth. This understanding would also better explain the view that Hyppolite's is a nonidealist, if not outright materialist, Hegel, although the role of Marxist dimensions of his reading (customarily used to justify this view) remains significant. In contrast to classical dialectical economies, however, I have in mind a more Nietzschean epistemology or antiepistemology, which is also antiontology or, in Heidegger's and Derrida's terms, antiontotheology. This point can also be brought into accord with what is seen as a more phenomenological (in the sense of Husserl and Heidegger) rather than idealist Hegel, which has emerged in Hyppolite's and other readings prior to structuralism and poststructuralism. As a result, a certain materialist phenomenology emerges as well, and, contrary to many (one might say, idealist) interpretations, such possibilities are suggested already by Husserl and Heidegger.

To borrow Deleuze's remarkable metaphors in *The Fold: Leibniz and the Baroque,* "the pleats of matter" and "the folds of the soul" continuously interact with, interfold, and pass into each other, and mix their curvatures—and there are no straight lines anywhere, either in Leibniz or in Hegel. Hegel, too, was a philosopher of the baroque—a philosopher of folding, unfolding, and interfolding matter and spirit. It is perhaps along these lines—these folds—that a new conjunction of Leibniz and Hegel, invoked by Hyppolite in 1966 in the context of formalism, will take place ("The Philosophical Language," 158); and Leibniz's and Hegel's are formalisms (if such is the term) of the fold, the nonformalizable formalism of the baroque. Deleuze's book may be more Hegelian and more Hyppolitean than Deleuze realized, or Hegel and Hyppolite may be more Deleuzean or more Leibnizian.

New conjunctions and mutual foldings of both philosophies with those of Kant and Spinoza emerge as well, via Nietzsche, whose philosophy of the future forms an irreducible mediation (to use Hegel's grand term *Vermittlung*) for everything in Deleuze. Or conversely, one might see

Nietzsche's philosophy as continuing or folded together with those of Hegel, Leibniz, and even Kant—arguably Nietzsche's greatest "enemy," along with Socrates. Nietzsche himself suggests such a possibility in *The Gay Science* when he speaks of three great insights defining German philosophy—"*Leibniz's* incomparable insight," "*Kant's* tremendous question mark," and "the astonishing stroke of *Hegel*." But then he refuses to see them as Germans. "[W]ere the German philosophers really philosophical *Germans*?"—he asks.[15] Perhaps, he sees them as (or translated into) philosophically *French*. Indeed Nietzsche may be brought closer to Socrates and Plato in this process, which can produce many other unorthodox, but (along unorthodox lines) logical and productive new conjunctions—for example, of Derrida and Deleuze, or Foucault, all students of Hyppolite.

New, unheard-of philosophical and political folds, and new, yet unattempted, translations and philosophies of the future may well be at stake. To have a chance to witness these tremendous struggles and transitions and, such is again their magic, by so doing also to take part in them is the greatest reason to read Hegel and Hyppolite.

Notes

1. For a useful historical background, see John Heckman's introduction to Hyppolite's *Genesis and Structure of Hegel's Phenomenology of Spirit*, trans. Samuel Cherniack and John Heckman (Evanston, Ill.: Northwestern University Press, 1974), xv–xli.

2. "The Discourse of Language," in *Archeology of Knowledge*, trans. A. M. Sheridan Smith (New York: Pantheon, 1971), 235.

3. Gilles Deleuze, *Empiricisme et subjectivité* (Paris: Presses Universitaires de France, 1953).

4. Martin Heidegger, *Hegel's Phenomenology of Spirit*, trans. Parvis Emad and Kenneth Maly (Bloomington: Indiana University Press, 1988), 424.

5. See, for example, *Beyond Good and Evil*, trans. Walter Kaufmann (New York: Vintage, 1966), 121–41.

6. *Inner Experience*, trans. Leslie Anne Boldt (Albany: State University of New York Press, 1980), 101.

7. *The Birth of Tragedy and the Case of Wagner*, trans. Walter Kaufmann (New York: Vintage, 1966), 97–98 (translation modified).

8. *Elements of the Philosophy of Right*, trans. N. B. Nisbet (Cambridge: Cambridge University Press, 1991), 371.

9. "The Structure of Philosophic Language According to the 'Preface' to Hegel's *Phenomenology of the Mind*," *The Languages of Criticism and the Sciences of Man: The Structuralist Controversy*, eds. Richard Macksey and Eugenio Donato (Baltimore: Johns Hopkins University Press, 1970), 169. This collection contains the essays presented at the 1966 conference at the Johns Hopkins University, one of the most significant events in recent

intellectual history, which brought together, among others, Hyppolite, Lacan, Barthes, Derrida, and de Man. The collection is dedicated to the memory of Hyppolite, who died in 1968.

10. See, for example, Gilles Deleuze and Clair Parnet, *Dialogues*, trans. Hugh Tomlinson and Barbara Habberjam (New York: Columbia University Press, 1987), 12–19.

11. *Hegel's Phenomenology of Spirit*, trans. A. V. Miller (Oxford: Oxford University Press, 1977), 492.

12. See, for example, Derrida's *Specters of Marx*, trans. Peggy Kamuf (New York: Routledge, 1994).

13. *Figures de la pensée philosophique* (Paris: Presses Universitaires de France, 1971), 360.

14. *On the Genealogy of Morals and Ecce Homo*, trans. Walter Kaufmann (New York: Vintage, 1967), 283.

15. *The Gay Science*, trans. Walter Kaufmann (New York: Vintage, 1974), 305.

Introduction

Hegelian Idealism

Lucien Herr wrote in the *Grande Encyclopédie:*[1] "Hegel's evolution was autonomous and completely personal. It is usually presented as a continuation and completion of the thought of Schelling, who had continued and developed the doctrine of Fichte who in turn was the continuator of Kant's thought. It may be that the conception of the successive value of these doctrines has schematic value, though certainly this does not pertain to historical truths." The relationship among Kant, Fichte, Schelling, and Hegel is, in fact, very fascinating. It undoubtedly accords with the interpretation that Hegel has given of himself in his history of philosophy, which is, as we know, a philosophy. It becomes a matter of historical interest when we know that Hegel considered himself the disciple of his friend Schelling (who was a fellow student at Tübingen with Hölderlin)[2] from the time of his arrival in Jena in 1801 to the publication of the *Phenomenology* in 1807. During the Jena years, Hegel, with the exception of his dissertation, *De Orbitis Planetarum* and his first work on *The Difference between the Systems of Fichte and Schelling,* published only some articles in Schelling's philosophical journal.[3] These articles, particularly the one entitled "Faith and Knowledge," have a very personal character, and we, who know the later Hegel of the *Phenomenology* and the earlier Hegel of the youthful works, can discover in them the originality of Hegelian thought, but this was not the case with his contemporaries. Hegel, before the publication of the *Phenomenology,* attempted to be no more than a disciple of Schelling, a rather obscure disciple who only endeavored to place Schelling's thought in the

mainstream of the philosophy of his time and to demonstrate the originality of this philosophy better than its author had done. Perhaps even Schelling
himself was indebted to his disciple and friend Hegel for being better
aware of the differences that existed between his philosophy of the absolute and the philosophies of reflection in Kant and Fichte. After the period
in which Hegel lived in the shadow of Schelling comes the great philosophic work of Hegel, the *Phenomenology*, which was completed, as we
know, at the moment of the battle of Jena and which for Hegel is a veritable
awakening of his own originality and a rather abrupt break with Schelling.
Especially in the preface of this work, Hegel reveals his own point of view
with lucidity and mastery. He opposes the romanticism of the followers of
Jacobi, Schleiermacher and Novalis, as well as the philosophy of Kant and
Fichte. But he is opposed with no less vigor to Schelling's philosophy of the
absolute, which is a philosophy of nature more than a philosophy of the
spirit; that is, a philosophy in which the history of peoples, the great
human drama, does not have its true place. To be sure, Schelling himself is
not named in this preface, but he could certainly recognize himself in it.[4]
From this moment on, Hegel's originality is no longer contested. In retro-
spectively considering this admirable philosophic movement that is German Idealism, Hegel can regard himself as the philosopher who has gone
beyond every attainment of this philosophic idealism, who has taken it to
its logical limit and expresses, so to speak, its dialectic result. Fichte represents subjective idealism, the eternal opposition of the self and nonself, an
unresolved opposition that ought to be resolved in a philosophy of moral
action.[5] Schelling represents objective idealism, the identity in the absolute
of the self and nonself, a philosophy of aesthetic contemplation. Hegel
advocates absolute idealism, preserving, in the center of the absolute, the
dialectic of reflection peculiar to Fichte, a philosophy of concrete synthesis.[6] We can therefore say that the vision that Hegel proposes is already to
an extent a philosophy of *The History of Philosophy* and that he has been the
first to create this presentation, though overly systematic, of three forms of
idealism, namely, subjective idealism, objective idealism, and absolute idealism, a representation by which we have frequently defined Hegelianism.

The discovery of Hegel's youthful writings, which remained unedited for a
long time and were published for the first time by Nohl in 1907, has
modified this representation profoundly.[7] In fact, these works must have
astonished those who know only the Hegel of the *Science of Logic* or the

Encyclopedia. Less astonished perhaps were those who had been aware of the concrete richness of Hegel's lectures on the philosophy of history, the philosophy of right, or aesthetics and religion. The study of the works of Hegel's youth was supposed to reveal two very neglected aspects of Hegelian thought. On the one hand, it was discovered that Hegel, who did not publish his masterpiece until he was thirty-five years old, had anticipated his entry upon the philosophical scene by a long initiation, a vast study of culture, and in the works published in his lifetime, he gave only the bare outline of a structure, with all the scaffoldings removed. On the other hand, we should be astonished that philosophy in the technical sense of the term occupies such a small place in these youthful notes. During the seminary years at Tübingen and the years of tutorship at Berne and Frankfurt, Hegel is concerned more with religious and historical problems than with strictly philosophical problems.[8] His correspondence with Schelling is proof of it. Immediately after his departure from Tübingen, Schelling abandons theological studies. Metaphysics becomes his exclusive concern, and he attempts to master Fichte's idealism by relating it to Spinoza's philosophy. He publishes *The Self as Principle of Philosophy*, then *Letters on Dogmatism and Criticism*, while Hegel remains very close to the concrete, the concrete being for him the life of peoples, and the spirit of Judaism and Christianity. He employs only philosophers, particularly Kant and ancient philosophers, so as better to approach his object directly, namely, human life as it is presented to him in history. More precisely, Hegel's preoccupations are of a practical order. Under the influence of the French Revolution (which momentarily enraptured him, as was the case with nearly all his contemporaries) he dreams of concrete reforms destined to revitalize some worm-eaten institutions.[9] In every case Hegel, as he writes to Schelling, has departed from the "most humble requirements of human thought." Only upon arriving at Jena does he become aware of philosophy as a means, perhaps more appropriate in our day than religion, of expressing the meaning of human life in its history.

But true philosophy, as Pascal has said, mocks philosophy, and Hegel's youthful works have the value of revealing to us the original starting point of Hegelian speculation. In our day, under the influence of Husserl, the German phenomenological school has wanted to substitute direct studies for secondary research, for example, in a philosophy of science that was only a science of science. The slogan of the new order has been "return to things themselves."[10] But this is exactly what is characteristic of Hegel's youthful works, which have been perhaps somewhat mistakenly called theological works. Hegel is less concerned there with technical philosophy than with history, and yet the word history is ill suited here to characterize this type of speculation. What is of interest to our thinker is the discovery of the spirit of a religion or the spirit of a people, and the invention of new concepts adequate to translate the historical life of man and its existence in a people or a history. On this point Hegel is incomparable, and the youthful works reveal to us his direct though naïve effort to think about human life. "To think about human life is the task,"[11] he writes. Only, this word "life" should not be understood to mean biological life, but life of the spirit inseparable from history. Yet it also should be added that Hegel seeks the meaning of this term "history" for the human spirit.

Before understanding Hegel as the successor of Fichte and Schelling and defining his philosophical position dialectically, it might be interesting to inquire as to what was the starting point of his thought and, by going back to the youthful works, to discover in them the fundamental nature of Hegelian Idealism. We could say that since the time of Dilthey this study of the youthful works has come a long way. It has renewed the interpretation of Hegelianism to the point of neglecting the final system a bit too much. It even seems that there is at times a sort of opposition between the interpreters of Hegel who are attached to his system as found in the *Encyclopedia* and those who remain faithful to the earliest formulations of Hegelian thought. While Kroner or Hartmann in their works on German Idealism neglect Hegel's youthful works and strive to understand our philosopher by locating him in the great philosophical stream of his time, Haering in Germany and Jean Wahl in France are more particularly interested in the phenomenological origin of the system, for example, those studies on the spirit of a people or on Christianity which are so animated and yet so undogmatic.[12]

We do not wish to choose one of these two ways exclusively here. Hegel's *Phenomenology* has particularly attracted us in our studies on Hegel, and this work is situated right between the youthful work that it reexamines and the future system that it proclaims. We find in it all of Hegel's "way of culture," which he himself has followed prior to reaching philosophy, and the prodigious effort of the logician to introduce this living experience within the limits of strict reflection. We do not need to know if logic has hardened this life or if, on the contrary, as Hegel wished, this life has not penetrated logic itself. Moreover, concerning this subject, we will have occasion to compare what Glockner calls the Hegelian *pantragicism* with his *panlogicism,* that is, his intuition of history with his theory of contradiction.[13]

Be that as it may, we will start with the youthful works of Hegel to better understand the meaning of the Hegelian system. We will not set the first in opposition to the second but will try to show that what constitutes Hegel's originality among the philosophers of German Idealism is already implicitly found in the works of Tübingen, Berne, and Frankfurt. A rapid comparison between Schelling and Hegel will make our thinking easier to understand.

Schelling, as Schiller had already done with regard to Kant, places Fichtean idealism, which is a moral idealism, in opposition to an idealism of aesthetic character. Intellectual intuition for Fichte, at least for the early Fichte, is that of moral action by which the free subject is raised to the highest consciousness of himself and, by completely setting himself in opposition to the world, denies the world. It is in this tension of the self, which is posited by opposing itself, that practical liberty resides. For Schelling, on the contrary, intellectual intuition, such as he presents at the end of his system of transcendental idealism, is an aesthetic intuition. The artist attains supreme freedom, not in a struggle but in a recovered harmony, that is, the coincidence with the absolute in aesthetic creation. The world of art gives us the highest revelation of the absolute.[14]

However, we do not find any philosophy of art in the earliest Hegelian works. By contrast, we find a meditation on the life of a people, on the living relation of the individual and the city as it is manifested to a Greek or a Roman. This object or this mirror, wherein the subject finds himself because he is its creation, is for Hegel from these first steps not nature or art, but spirit known as *supraindividual* reality, as spirit of a people or spirit of a religion. The experience of historical totalities is doubtless Hegel's fundamental experience, the one he is going to attempt to integrate into German Idealism. The Kantian theory of freedom, developed so profoundly by Fichte, was still an abstract theory. Philosophical Idealism needed to think of man in his concrete history and to find his spirit therein. Schiller, Goethe, and Schelling had opened the way for this, but they considered (as Goethe must have done) the problem of the relations of spiritual man and nature above all. They raised themselves to a thought of art rather than to a thought of the history of peoples, as already foreseen by Herder.

It is, on the contrary, this thought of history from which Hegel started, and it is this that is found again in the masterly works of his philosophic career from the *Phenomonology* in 1807 to the *Philosophy of Right* in 1821. The study of Hegel's youthful works will lead us therefore from the first thought about the spirit of a people (*Volksgeist*) to the problem of historical development by the intermediary of the notions of *positivity* and *destiny*. Afterward we will see how Hegel, during the years of appropriate philosophical cultivation at Jena, will organize these notions and attempt to present them conceptually in a first philosophy of right and in a first ethical system, which remained unpublished during his life. These notions are the intuition of the organic life of a people and its relation to the history of the spirit of the world. In this domain of the spirit, Hegel's studies are, as we have said, a firsthand work, but in the field of the philosophy of nature, he does not think about things themselves. He does not have, as Schelling does, any intuition or any cosmic sympathies. He confines himself to reflecting upon the concepts of philosophy of nature, which he borrows from his old classmate. He thinks about the concepts that this philosophy of nature has already somewhat directly elaborated, just as a philosophy of science deals with concepts that science has given it. It is not the same in the field of human history. Here Hegel elaborates concepts by beginning with their very source, but this formation of the first fundamental concepts of Hegelian philosophy is most important in order to understand this philosophy. That is why we will study these concepts with reference to their origin by addressing the youthful works.

I

The Spirit of a People (*Volksgeist*)

"Happy," wrote Hölderlin in *Hyperion,* "is the man who draws his joy and his strength from the welfare of his native land."[1] For Hegel the individual, reduced to himself, is only an abstraction. That is why for him true organic unity, the concrete universal, is the people. While Schelling sees in the production of the work of art absolute intuition, that is, that which reconciles subject and object, the conscious and the unconscious, Hegel, in writing the *System der Sittlichkeit* at Jena, substitutes the concrete organism of the life of a people for the work of art as the expression of the absolute. His first philosophy of spirit will be the description of social organization from its foundations in the concrete needs of men to its highest expression in the state, the religion of the people, an original spiritual greatness simultaneously subjective and objective. In the family, the highest unity in which nature left to itself is exalted, "man sees the flesh of his flesh in woman," but this contemplation of himself in another, simultaneously identical and different, is still affected by a natural difference. The family is only an anticipation of the spirit of a people, and that is why Hegel adds, "If by nature man sees the flesh of his flesh in woman, by the ethical order he discovers the spirit of his spirit in and through ethical reality."[2] It is in and only in a people that morality is realized, since morality is no longer only an ought-to-be, "an inaccessible ideal." If one considers the spirit of a people as spiritual reality or second nature, as Schelling had already said in speaking about the world of right, it can be said that "reason is actually realized" and is "the presence of living spirit." The individual has in this spirit not only his *destination,* but also his realization. He is not beyond it since it is present in the morals and whole life of his people. That is why the sages of antiquity have said that wisdom and virtue consist in living in conformity with the customs of one's people.[3]

The spirit of a people is thus what reconciles the ought-to-be and reality. This is a historical reality which goes infinitely beyond the individual, but which allows him to find himself in an objective form. This is truly the world of spirit (the individual who is a world, as Hegel says in the *Phenomenology*) and not in the state as the ideal as it is in the moral philosophy of Kant and Fichte, for whom the world, even the spiritual world, "is always as it ought not to be, so that morality causes it to be as it ought to be." But Hegel investigates beyond morality (*Moralität*), which according to Kant and Fichte expresses only the point of view of the acting individual, the living reality of morals and institutions (*Sittlichkeit*). Virtue, in the present sense of the term, has a clearly individualistic meaning. It corresponds to the moment of opposition between the individual and his people. "It was not like ancient virtue which was a substantial virtue,"[4] which found its content in the very life of the people. In order to make the very important distinction which Hegel makes here between the terms *Moralität* and *Sittlichkeit,* we shall adopt the expressions "morality" and "ethical world" as a practice. The choice of the word "ethical" is of course rather arbitrary, but it has the advantage of being connected etymologically to the Greek term *ethos* (custom, use), which Hegel considers as being equivalent to the German term *Sitte.* Doubtless the word "morality" is also connected to *mores,* but this inevitable etymology certainly indicates that morality in the Kantian sense of the term is only a part, and not the whole, of ethical life. It corresponds only to the stage of subjective reflection and is situated between the immediate life in a people and the objective organization of society and state.[5]

These remarks would lead us, if we developed them, beyond Hegel's first intuitions to the system realized in his *Philosophy of Right,* but it is of more interest now for us to seek the origin of his thought. Now it is indubitable that starting with his first youthful works, particularly those at Tübingen, Hegel thinks of the spiritual life as the life of a people. The terms that he employs during this period are characteristic in this regard. He speaks of the spirit of a people (*Volksgeist*), the soul of a people (*Seele des Volks*), the genius of a people (*Genius des Volks*). We will soon look at the origins of these expressions in the philosophy of the time, but they already clearly indicate one of the characteristic aspects of Hegelian thought. Between individualism and cosmopolitanism, Hegel seeks concrete spirit as the spirit of a people. The incarnation of spirit is a reality both individual and universal as it is presented in the history of the world in the form of a people. Humanity is realized only in the various peoples who express in their unique way their universal character.[6]

However, Hegel's first works bear especially upon religion. But to be precise, religion is one of the essential moments of the genius and spirit of a people, and as such Hegel is going to try to consider it. Thereby he will certainly be opposed to the abstract and antihistorical conception that the eighteenth century has made of it in the name of natural religion. But neither will he accept (although his development in this regard is rather complex) the pure moralism of Kant, which postulates religion emanating from the pure moral ideal. In short, in attempting to take a middle ground in the midst of these various conceptions, Hegel will deepen his own thought of religion and at the same time his idea, which is more historical than that of the philosophers of the eighteenth century, of the spirit of a people.

During his years at the seminary at Tübingen, Hegel is, like his classmates Schelling and Hölderlin, sensitive to the beauty of classical antiquity. The Greek city is for them the happy city, the youthfulness of the world, where the individual lives in perfect harmony with the whole to which he is integrated. A concrete ideal of humanity has been realized, but western peoples have lost this happiness. In the seventeenth century Christianity is no more than an external religion, which does not penetrate profoundly enough into the life of souls. Hegel is also aware of the great movement of rationalistic liberation that has appeared in France and is spreading in Germany in the name of the *Aufklärung*. He knows French philosophers of the eighteenth century. He reads Rousseau with passion, and he studies Montesquieu, whose writing he will later describe as "immortal work."[7] In this atmosphere his own thought is formed, and we can already attempt to characterize, as early as this era, the theoretical and practical problem that is the heart of the matter.

Hegel wonders under what condition a religion can live.[8] It is in this way he distinguishes, taking his inspiration from Rousseau, a *subjective* religion from an *objective* religion. Subjective religion, which resembles the religion of the Savoyard vicar, is opposed at the same time to the dry and abstract rationalism of a Voltaire and the positive theology of an authoritarian religion. It is a religion of the heart, capable, Hegel says, "of inspiring the greatest actions because it affects the entire man and not just his unaided reason." Objective religion, on the contrary, "allows itself to be organized intellectually. It allows itself to be systematized, to be formalized in a book, to be conveyed verbally to others; subjective religion is externalized only in feelings and acts."[9] Let us note this last expression, "subjective religion is externalized in acts." It is sufficient to know the later Hegel, the one for whom "the true reality of man is his action" or the one for whom "the history of the world is the judgment of the world," in order to understand the importance of this remark. In his first studies on religion, which should lead to the ideal of the religion of a people, Hegel wants to find concrete man whose negative reflection upon life causes him to distinguish too arbitrarily the faculties such as reason and sensibility. But concrete man *may not know how* to be purely individual, isolated from his fellow creatures and, if one may say so, from his spiritual environment. That is why Hegel puts *religion of a people* in opposition to *private religion.* This second opposition is more important than the preceding one for it shows us the supraindividualistic meaning of Hegel's first works. From this early period religion appears, according to Hegel, as one of the most important manifestations of the spirit of a people. "Religion is one of the most important things in human life. It frames the life of a people." "The spirit of the people, history, religion, and the degree of political freedom of this people, are not to be considered in isolation, but are united in an indissolvable way."[10] It is remarkable that Hegel's first meditations do not proceed from morality to religion by following the path outlined by Kant in the *Critique of Practical Reason* or in the *Religion within the Limits of Pure Reason.* On the contrary, he studies religion and sees it expressing human life more concretely than an abstract moralism could.[11] But Christianity especially is a private religion, as Rousseau had already noted. On the other hand, ancient religion is a religion of the city, an intuition that people have of the absolute reality of religion. The religion of a people and private religion are opposed, as Hellenism and Christianity, and Hegel declares himself at first against the individualism of his time, whose parenthood he attributes at times to Christianity. In a study of Hegel's years at Tübingen we have been able to suggest certain relations, on the one hand, between private religion and what Hegel will call later *Moralität*, and, on the other hand, between the religion of a people and *Sittlichkeit*, ethical rule, or the morals of a people.[12]

By placing subjective religion in opposition to objective religion, the religion of a people in opposition to private religion, Hegel adopts an attitude regarding religion that is different from the *Aufklärung*. Whereas the abstract rationalism of the *Aufklärung* dissolves every form of religious life and leads either to atheism or to a natural religion without life and concrete content, Hegel tries to understand a religion as one of the primal manifestations of the genius of a particular people. That is why for him the formation of the spirit of a people is connected to its religion, to ceremonies and myths that abstract understanding cannot comprehend by isolating them from their environment and depriving them of their original meaning. A completely different interpretation of religion than that of the eighteenth century is revealed here. But cannot the seeds of it already be found in Herder? "Adapting oneself," says Hegel, "to the religion of a people through the understanding is not the way to know it."

Religion therefore is for Hegel a supraindividualistic phenomenon. It relates to that unique and singular totality that is the spirit of a people. But what exactly does this mean in Hegel's first works?

It is difficult to give it a very exact meaning, and a long philosophic development will be necessary before Hegel strictly defines what he understands to be the spirit of a people and before he considers philosophy of history as the development of the spirit of the world through these particular moments that are the spirits of individual peoples. At the beginning of these meditations it is more a question of an intuition than a well-defined concept. The essential thing appears to us to be this idea that the whole that constitutes a people is not the result of a combination. In Aristotle, the whole is prior to its parts. In our day we like to put the concepts of *community* and *society* in opposition, but this opposition is found already sketched in the first stages of Hegelian thought. Society is made up of an association of individuals who have a particular end in view. The group is not in itself its own end. On the contrary, in the community the unity of individuals comes first; it is the immanent *Τέλος*. The spirit of a people for Hegel is much more what expresses a spiritual community than what results from a contract along the lines of civil contracts. This spirit of a people is in sum an original spiritual reality having a unique and indivisible character. It is already an Idea, in the sense that Hegel himself will later give to this term. Therefore the notion of the spirit of a people is opposed, in the earliest Hegelian speculations, to the atomistic conceptions of the eighteenth century.[13] A people is not made up of individual atoms; rather, it is an organization (Hegel will strongly insist on this point) that preexists in its members. Finally, the spirit of a people in Hegel's youthful thinking is not opposed to individual spirits. There is, on the contrary, a necessarily preestablished harmony among them. The individual can be completely realized only by participating in what both transcends him and expresses him in a family, a culture, and a people. Only as such is he *free*.

We may wonder from whom Hegel has borrowed his expressions of "spirit" and "genius" of a people. We think first of all of Montesquieu, whom Hegel had especially studied and to whom he refers several times. According to Montesquieu, the investigation of general laws does not exclude the study of differences and specifics. In seeking the *spirit of laws* Montesquieu wanted to discover the relationships that laws have with the geographic environment or with "the general spirit of a nation." "Laws," he writes, "ought to be so appropriate to the people for whom they are made that it is a very great accident if those of one nation can agree with another."[14] But according to him the spirit of a people appears as a result of various forces. Later, on the contrary, for the historical school, the spirit of a people will be like an original germ, a first basic idea. Hegel already rises above this opposition by particularly defining the spirit of a people by its spiritual factors. Even in his future philosophy of history, which contains such interesting remarks on the geographic distribution of civilizations, natural forces will play only a subordinate role. They will be mere conditions for the manifestation of a certain spirit. However, it is not true that Hegel ignores the connection between nature and the spirit of a people. In a youthful fragment, he writes in the form of a poetic myth: "The spirit of a people is connected to the earth by a slight tie, but one which almost magically resists every attempt to break it, for it is completely self-contained."[15]

Be that as it may, the characterization that Hegel makes of the spirit of a people is different from what Montesquieu calls the general spirit of a nation. He seeks to seize the irreducible originality of an individual spirit rather than to discover mechanical components.[16] On this point he is nearer to his contemporary and compatriot Herder than to the French philosopher. In fact, in Herder, the primitive genius of people is considered for the first time in conjunction with a "historical consciousness." Also, during their Strasbourg conversations, Herder had caused Goethe to discover the dimension of history, by making him understand the primitive poetry of people as well as the Bible or Shakespeare; Herder's action also must have been important to Hegel. Herder looked for vital energy everywhere in history, not the static kind, but developmental, the sign of acting force. But his conception of development was still a bit too naturalistic to inspire the Hegelian conception. Hegel, in order to describe the life of the spirit and particularly the life of people in history, will initially make use of organic metaphors, but he will progressively substitute a dialectic that is better adapted to spiritual development.

Finally it is necessary to note an influence that certainly has been very important, namely Rousseau's. That can appear initially paradoxical. We in France are often tempted to interpret the *Social Contract* as an individualistic work because the State is considered to be a result of a contract between individuals. But in fact it was not the contract, as contract, that especially was striking to Hegel, but the idea of *general will.* There is a certain transcendence of general will in individual wills, and the consideration of the state as will is the great discovery of Rousseau for Hegel. Hegel does not say "that the act of association produces a moral and collective body which receives from this very act its unity, its common self, its life and its will."[17] Finally, it is Rousseau himself who insisted on the difference between the general will and the will of all: "The general will considers only common interest; the other considers only private interest, and is only a sum of particular wills." Hegel therefore found in Rousseau the idea of the general will of a people, which is both the ideal for individuals and reality in the sovereign. "The sovereign, by virtue of what he is, is always all he ought to be."[18] Furthermore, Rousseau sees in the general will of an individual people a particular will in regard to other peoples. Therefore, his conception must have inspired in Hegel many of the characteristics of his own thought. The notion of contract remains tainted with individualism; it still starts from an atomistic prejudice. That is why Hegel will be led to criticize it, but by insisting more clearly on the essential idea of general will, different from particular wills.

We can grasp these various influences on the formation of the first Hegelian concept of the spirit of a people. But the Hegelian conception is no less original, as we hope to show in the remainder of this study. However, before viewing the Hegelian thought of history made more definite by his discussion of the ideas of "positivity" and "destiny," it would be of interest for us to investigate what was at the beginning of his formation, namely, the Hegelian idea of Freedom. This idea of Freedom (a certain harmonious relationship of the individual and the City, an active participation of man in his terrestrial city) was a characteristic of the ancient world for our philosopher. Its disappearance and the birth of a sort of separation into two worlds joined to Christianity are characteristics of the unhappy consciousness.[19]

II

The First Form of the
Unhappy Consciousness

Freedom in the Ancient World and in Christianity

Dilthey was the first to note the importance of a text of Hegel's youth and noted it to be a first outline of what would later be the concept of the "unhappy consciousness." We know of the importance of the unhappy consciousness in Hegel's *Phenomenology* and still later in the *Philosophy of Religion*. In abstract form the unhappy consciousness is the consciousness of the contradiction between man's finite life and his thought of the infinite. "By thinking I raise myself to the absolute in transcending everything finite. I am therefore an infinite consciousness and at the same time I am a consciousness of finite self by my every empirical determination. . . . The two limits both seek each other and flee from each other. I am the feeling, intuition, representation of this unity and this conflict, and the conjunction of these limits in conflict . . . I am this combat. I am not one of these limits engaged in the conflict, but I am the two combatants and the combat itself. I am fire and water which enter into contact, and I am the contact and unity of what absolutely avoids each other."[1] The unhappy consciousness, which in the *Phenomenology* finds its historical incarnation in Judaism and in a part of the Christian Middle Ages, is in fact the consciousness of life as unhappiness of life.[2] Man is raised above his terrestrial and mortal condition. He is no more than the conflict of the infinite and finite, of the absolute that he has posited outside of life and of his life reduced to finitude. The conflict is the expression of Romanticism and the philosophy of Fichte, the expression of the tragedy of the Self. It is one of the essential moments of Hegelian philosophy, one that responds to rending and division and that precedes every unification and reconciliation.

That is why it is all the more interesting to look for the first form of the unhappy consciousness in the study of a historical crisis. What appears remarkable to us is that Hegel has not begun by thinking of the unhappy consciousness in its general form, namely, as the conflict between the infinite and finite in man, a fact particularly illustrated by the text that we have just cited. On the contrary, by considering a historical evolution, the passage from the ancient world to the modern world, he has presented for the first time this division of human consciousness. Moreover, if in the *Phenomenology* unhappy consciousness is presented in this abstract and general form in the course of the development of the consciousness of the self, it is also presented once more in the course of the development of the spirit (understood as supraindividualistic reality)[3] and precisely with regard to the disappearance of the ancient city at the moment when the Roman Empire allows individuals to be dissolved into their particularity by according them no more than an appearance of universality, that of Roman law. Therefore, we are going to study more particularly that text from Berne with the aim of uncovering in it a first form of historical dialectic and the origin of what will be for Hegel the unhappiness of consciousness. The text is entitled: "The Difference between Greek Religious Imagination and Christian Positive Religion."[4] The problem that Hegel raises is the transition from the ancient world to the modern Christian world. The readings that have inspired our philosopher are those of Montesquieu and above all Gibbon. But the way he treats this is particularly original. This treatment concerns the characterization of an evolution of the human spirit, the imperceptible passage from one world of the spirit to another world of the spirit. Hegel does not stop with the historical event; he seeks to understand it profoundly and discover an evolution of values in a shifting of institutions: "The repression of pagan religion by the Christian religion is one of the most astonishing revolutions, and investigation into its causes ought to concern the philosopher of history more."[5] The great revolutions, those that are striking to everyone, Hegel tells us, ought to be perceived as preceded by silent revolutions "which are not visible to everyone nor observable by their contemporaries and which are as difficult to formulate as to understand." It is the misunderstanding of such internal transformations in the social body and in life and morals that afterward makes these revolutions that appear abruptly on the scene of the world so astonishing. Likewise, Hegel will say in the *Phenomenology* that the birth of a child, the abrupt qualitative leap, is preceded by a slow formation, by an imperceptible quantitative development.[6] To grasp these transformations of the spirit of the world and to adapt thought to this spiritual development is Hegel's initial purpose. Did he not assist in his day in bringing about transformations of this very kind? His dialectic, prior to being logical, is first of all an effort of thought to apprehend historical development and to reconcile time and concept. Now the transition from the ancient city, the ideal of Hegel's youth, to the modern world and to his own religion, namely, Christianity, cannot be explained in a simple way. "How," says Hegel, "could a religion disappear which for centuries had been rooted in States, which had such a close connection to the constitution of the State?"[7] Today we consider the divinities and the pagan mysteries as unworthy of any belief. Their absurdity seems obvious, and yet the best men of antiquity adhered to what seems to us a fabric of silliness. But Hegel justly remarks that we do not find in the ancients requirements "which are those of our present-day practical reason." The idea of an evolution of practical reason that would be so strange to a Kant, the idea of its dependence upon history, is therefore manifested clearly here.

Be that as it may, our completely intellectual explanation of the passage from paganism to Christianity is insufficient. It might have been sufficient that the understanding enlightens pagan myths to discover the childishness in them, but the pagans also had an understanding. The abstract and general explanation of the *Aufklärung* would not be able to content us. There is a spiritual transformation in understanding as such: "Whoever has already made these remarks will not be satisfied by this answer." Therefore, it is necessary to understand, contrary to the completely political and artificial explanation of a Montesquieu, how the religion of the Greeks and Romans was connected with all ancient life. It was not a metaphysical system, a product of reflection, but it was bound up with the life of the citizen, with wars, and with constitutions. Originally it was a religion of a people and was not imposed externally upon citizens who participated in it. "The religion of Greece and Rome was a religion for free peoples, and meaning also must have disappeared with loss of freedom, along with the power of this religion and its adaptation to human life."[8] The transformation from freedom to despotism brought about the decline of ancient religion. It lost its power over people when liberty became an empty word: "What use are the nets to the fisherman if the current has dried up?"

The disappearance of paganism would therefore be bound up with the disappearance of freedom. At first Hegel's explanation appears misleading. What freedom was it and what did it consist of? Toward the end of his life Hegel would write concerning freedom: "The final end of the world is consciousness of the freedom of the spirit. But only in our time has the indeterminency of this freedom such as we have described been better known and proven."[9] In other words, the very concept of freedom would need explaining. It is certainly difficult for us to admit that the citizen of antiquity enjoyed what for us is individual freedom, such as freedom of conscience. But for the young Hegel, freedom is not free will of the individual. Rather, this freedom refers to a harmonious relationship between the individual and his city: "The idea of his native country or his State was invisible reality for the citizen of antiquity, the most elevated thing for which he labored. It was his final purpose of the world or the final purpose of his world."[10] Hegel recalls Montesquieu, for whom the principle of the republic was virtue, not in the sense of an individualistic morality, but of civic morality. The citizen of antiquity was free just because *his private life* was not set in opposition to *his public life*. He belonged to the city, but the city was not like a State, a foreign power that coerced him. "As a free man he obeyed laws which he had given himself. He sacrificed his property, his passions, his life for a reality which was his own."[11] Therefore this freedom was an integration of the individual to the whole, and to a whole, to an *idea*, as Hegel already said, that was present for him in reality and not in a beyond. The native land or city was not a mere thing for the citizen of antiquity but a living reality. There had been no division in this life. The individual was not opposed to the State, which would cause him, left on his own, to seek his highest good in a beyond. Ancient religion was only the expression of this life. "In the presence of this idea," said Hegel, "his individuality disappeared." He put the eternal part of himself in his city. That is why the problem of the immortality of the soul was not posed for him in the same way as for us: "Cato only turned to Plato's *Phaedo* when the order of highest things such as his world, his republic, was broken for him. Then he fled toward an order of things still higher."[12] We understand that for Hegel Plato's *Republic* was not a utopia; rather, it interpreted the immanent ideal in the ancient city conceptually.[13]

What transformation was produced in this ancient world? Hegel will say later in the *Phenomenology* that the municipal system is at base under the influence of wars. Imperialism has appeared and with it the falling back of the individual on himself. Increasing wealth and inequality have entailed the dissolution of the State: "Soon we will be a witness to the loss of that feeling, that consciousness that Montesquieu, in the name of virtue, considered to be the principle of the republic, and that capacity of sacrificing the individual for an idea which, for the republican, is realized in his native land."[14]

Henceforth we witness a decadence, and this disappearance of the living connection between the citizen and his city will engender new needs and lead to one of the most important transformations of history. "The image of the State as a product of his activity disappeared from the soul of the citizen."[15] Only a few bore the burden of the State, at times only a single one. Others were no more than gears in a machine.[16] That is why what was freedom for Hegel disappeared and in its place rose the limited interest of the individual for himself, an activity that was no longer free in itself since it was finite and encountered its limits everywhere. "Every activity and every goal was related only to the individual; there was no longer any activity for the whole, that is, for an idea."[17] In place of this integration to a life, which was the life of his city, the individual turns back upon himself and is concerned with his own pleasure. The lust for private property gives Hegel a clue to this transformation. Wealth replaced the State, and this transformation appears so important to Hegel that he will make it a recurring evolution of the spirit. *State* and *Wealth* will be found again in the courses on the philosophy of the spirit at Jena and in the *Phenomenology* as two moments of a dialectic.[18] Property and the relation of owners among themselves become the essential thing while private right or abstract right are constituted. Each citizen can consider the State only as a foreign power that he uses to the best of his interests. "Each works for himself or by compulsion for another individual." The right of the citizen no longer implies merely a right to the security of property; the latter now fills the whole life of the individual.[19] In the *Phenomenology* Hegel will return to this Roman law life that is substituted for the ethical life of the city. This law is essentially individualistic; it is no longer the old self-evident religious law. It takes on a universal character, and the individual is certainly recognized. But what is recognized in him is the abstract person, the mask of the living and concrete man. No more than a social atomism exists.

Henceforth ancient religion no longer has any meaning. New demands are sensed in this unhappiness of the world, and Christianity, which is called by Hegel a private religion at Tübingen, can be established. Since what filled man's life and his activity disappears for him, "death should have appeared frightening to him for nothing survived him any longer. To the republican, on the contrary, the republic survived." In this state man should flee the world to find something absolute outside of it. The finite and the infinite should have been separated for him, and God should have appeared as an inaccessible beyond. "Reason could not renounce finding the absolute somewhere, the independent which one could not encounter in the will of man. It appeared in the divinity that the Christian religion offered him outside human power and will, but not, however, outside human supplication and prayer."[20] The realization of a moral idea could therefore still only be desired but not willed (for what we can desire, we cannot ourselves accomplish; rather, we wait for it without our cooperation). The passivity of man is accompanied by this requirement whose limit was beyond. Hegel insists again on the character of this torn humanity, incapable of sacrificing its life for a native land, for the taste for security and individual peace had become too general. "We no longer take any interest in the State since we are no longer really active in it, for we can take interest only in a thing in which we are active. We only passively hope that it will be maintained to assure us our daily bread or the excesses to which we are accustomed. We absent ourselves from every war because it is contrary to the general will, namely, the need for a calm and monotonous pleasure." But for Hegel war is a necessary moment of the life of a people, and the people who are not capable of sustaining it are no longer a free people.

We see by these various citations what freedom means here for Hegel (the opposite of an individual free will) and what for our philosopher contributes to a historically happy people. In this demise of the city the unhappy consciousness appears, and Christianity is an expression of it. But Hegel does not return to what is past. This great rending has its necessity, and the unhappy consciousness is a necessary division so that a reunification may be possible. The problem that is posed for him at this moment is the following: how to recover this harmonious relation of the individual to his city, through the contemporary rending, a rending for which Christianity is particularly responsible.

III

Reason and History

The Ideas of Positivity and Destiny

1. The Idea of Positivity

Hegel's philosophy consummates the philosophy of the eighteenth century and initiates the philosophy of the nineteenth; it is the hinge of two eras. This judgment is confirmed if we consider the position that Hegel takes toward History and Reason. Reason and History, we may say, are the two terms that he envisages to oppose or conciliate each other, as far back as his youthful writings, more particularly during the period of Berne and Frank- furt. The two fundamental studies of these periods are, in addition to a *Life of Jesus,* a writing on the *Positivity of the Christian Religion* and another on the *Spirit of Christianity and Its Destiny.*[1] Here the two key concepts to retain, around which all his meditations converge, are the concepts of positivity and destiny. Their meanings, at first trite, are progressively enriched. With these concepts, Hegel approaches the problem of the relationship of reason and history. At first he poses this problem with some subtle differences about man of the eighteenth century, but he resolves this problem in man of the nineteenth century. A historical reason is manifested at the end of these studies, a reason that is concretely enriched in history, as history is enlightened by reason.[2]

Let us consider first of all the term "positivity" and see what it means for Hegel. The opposition with *natural religion* is trivial in this era, and it is certainly relevant to religion that Hegel speaks of positivity. But the term has a larger application, and during the Jena period Hegel will be able to apply, *mutatis mutandis,* the result of his first works to the opposition: positive right—natural right.[3] In the eighteenth century positive religion was put in opposition to natural religion. "The concept of positivity of a religion has only taken birth and become important in contemporary times."[4] This opposition is presented because it is presupposed that there is a human nature and a natural religion corresponding to it, whereas we recognize in history a multitude of various religions that all diverge more or less by their institutions, ceremonies, and fundamental beliefs. Let us consider, for example, the position of a rationalist such as Voltaire in regard to religions. He reduces the beliefs that reason can admit to their simplest terms, namely, *the existence of God and the immortality of the soul,* and tends to consider as aberrations all religions that have been manifested in history and have added their superstitions to a rational foundation, a foundation Voltaire only appears to tolerate in matters of belief. A positive religion is therefore a historical religion. It adds to what human reason, reduced to itself alone, can give, beliefs that have appeared at a given moment in time, in certain places in space, and beliefs that could not be fully assimilated by reason, that come from other sources. We can therefore say with Hegel of positive religions that they are "either supernatural or antinatural." For example, a Christian acknowledges a particular revelation of God that constitutes a reality irreducible to pure thought, a sort of irrational that is both a given for reason and a historical phenomenon. If we master ever so little the problem of positivity, we discover the philosophic problem of realism and idealism. What is the positive, in fact, if it is not the given, or what appears to be imposed outside of reason? And that given being a historical given, the question raised here is that of the relations of reason and history like that of the irrational and the rational.

If we no longer consider this problem in its theoretical aspect but in its practical aspect, we will discover yet another opposition included in it, that of *constraint* and *freedom,* and it is this last opposition that we think is important to the reader of the *Critique of Practical Reason* and the *Religion within the Limits of Pure Reason.* "A positive religion," Hegel says, "implies feelings that are more or less impressed by constraint on the sensibilities; these are actions which are the effect of a commandment and the result of an obedience and are accompanied without direct interest."[5] In other words, in a positive religion there is an externality for practical reason. Man is not free but submits to a law that he has not given to himself. In the same way as for theoretical reason, the positive represents what is imposed outside of thought and what thought ought to receive passively. Likewise, the positive represents for practical reason an order and implies between God and Man a relation of master to slave. But Kant's great idea, which goes well beyond the dull rationalism of the *Aufklärung* but which nevertheless is the supreme expression of it, is that reason is practical by itself. The highest requirement of man is to be free, that is, to owe only to himself the rule of his action. The idea of freedom and the idea of autonomy are the key concepts of the critique of practical reason. If, on the other hand, Kant speaks of having limited reason in order to make place for faith, it is not a question of understanding by this the acceptance of something irrational in the field of pure reason. The law that Kant admits is a moral law; it does not make any appeal to history or to a particular revelation. Pure freedom (autonomy) and the situation of man caught between this freedom and nature certainly lead us to postulates that can be admitted by reason without contradiction, but these postulates are only the existence of God and the immortality of the soul (derived from an indefinite progress possible in morality). There is nothing in this that goes beyond natural religion, if we mean by natural religion a religion that can be admitted by reason, always self-identical and thus nontemporal.[6] Kant wrote *Religion within the Limits of Pure Reason* and encountered even before Hegel the problem of positivity, but he discarded it. Christ appears there only as a model of morality, a scheme by which we can make ourselves sensitive to the moral ideal that reason offers us. Any other conception of Christianity would result in making freedom disappear, by transforming *morality* into *legalism*. This opposition, which Kant has insisted on so much and Hegel will later strive to transcend, is still useful to us to understand the meaning that Hegel places on the problem of positivity. Legality is heteronomy; it is obedience by compulsion to a law that goes beyond us and that does not come from us. Morality is freedom itself or autonomy. We only follow a single law, one that we find in ourselves and that is our own. To be autonomous is to become greater and not to submit passively to a foreign order. For Hegel the most striking example of legalism is Judaism, the obedience to laws that divinity has imposed on man. Man only submits because he fears God, a God who is beyond him and whose slave he is. A positive religion is therefore, from the point of view of practical reason, a religion that is based on authority and that, by treating man as a child, imposes on him externally what is not contained in his reason. Positive religion makes God a master, but it makes man a slave and cultivates in him the feeling of slavery. The concepts of constraint and authority that appear here are antithetical to freedom, but that authority, not being based on human reason (in which case we could no longer speak of constraint), can be connected only with a temporal event, with a historical relation. That is why Hegel, summing up these various meanings of positivity, can say, "This historical element in general is called authority."[7]

Therefore, we see the complexity of the questions that are raised related to this concept of positivity, and Hegel's successive attempts to connect dialectically (a dialectic that is not yet conscious of itself) *pure reason* (theoretical and especially practical) and positivity, that is, *the historical element.* In a certain sense Hegel considered positivity as an obstacle to the freedom of man, and as such it is condemned. To investigate the positive elements of a religion, and we could add, of a social state, is to discover what is imposed by constraint on man, what blemishes the purity of reason, which in another sense ends up by involving positivity in the course of Hegel's development. Positivity ought to be reconciled with reason, which then loses its abstract character and becomes appropriate to the concrete richness of life. Therefore, we see why the concept of positivity is in the center of Hegelian perspectives.[8]

First of all, Hegel, by reviving Kant's study on *Religion within the Limits of Pure Reason,* tries to set Christ in opposition to Judaism, as the partisan of moral autonomy to a people who have known only legalism and separateness. But what a difference there already is between this life of Jesus and Kant's work! Jesus is no longer just a sensible scheme, a representation of the ideal of morality. He is an individual, and it is a real history that Hegel strives to retrace. It is a historical story; Jesus is certainly the moral ideal, but he is presented as a living being. However, it is the opposition of autonomy to heteronomy that characterizes Christ's teaching and life. "As you revere as your highest law the ordinances of the church and the laws of the State, you misunderstand the dignity and power in man to create for himself the concept of divinity."[9] Pure Kantian rationalism still seems to be the inspiration for this text: "Reason is what makes man know his destination, the unconditional purpose of his life. Certainly reason is often eclipsed, but reason can never be completely extinct. Even in the midst of darkness there always remains a feeble glimmer." The story finally ends with the death of Christ. It speaks neither of his miracles nor of his resurrection.[10]

In spite of this criticism of all positivity and of this life of Jesus, which is the first of the century that appears negative about every transcendence, we would be wrong to believe that Hegelian rationalism is of the same essence as Kantian rationalism. Many passages on love and life already indicate a distinct orientation in this work. For Hegel the essential opposition is not between pure reason and the empirical element, but rather the opposition between life and nonlife or between the living and the dead. In this sense the verdict concerning the positivity of a religion is no longer so simple. At the end of the Berne period Hegel contrasts the abstract concepts of human reason, those of the *Aufklärer,* and the modalities of life. In order to contrast positive religion and natural religion, it is necessary to be able to define once and for all the concept of human nature, that is, the requirements of human reason reduced to itself. But we have already seen in reference to a text on the transition from paganism to Christianity that the needs of practical reason were possibly not the same for people of antiquity as they are for us. Here Hegel writes: "But living nature is eternally something other than the concept of this nature and thus what for the concept was only modification, pure contingence and a superfluity, becomes the necessary, the living, perhaps the only natural and only beautiful thing."[11] In other words, these abstract ideas of human nature, these concepts of pure reason, are incapable of furnishing here the standard of measure that would show in a religion, as in a social world, what is positive and what is not. Measure is impossible: "The general concepts of human nature are too empty to be able to give a standard for the particular and necessarily diverse requirements of religiosity." No longer by reason does Hegel judge the positive but rather by relation to life, and in the development of his thought during the Frankfurt period this idea of life is going to become dominant in his reflection. The positive, in the pejorative sense of the word, will not be the concrete, historical element that is intimately connected to the development of a religion or a society, which makes contact with them and, therefore, is not imposed outside of them. It will be only the dead element, which has lost its living meaning and is no more than a residue of history. The figure of Christ in Hegel's studies becomes more and more concrete. What is positive in religion that has abandoned its prophesy is connected to what formerly was living and what depends strictly on its historical individuality. The very person of Christ furnishes the positive datum: he teaches and acts; he speaks on the basis of his own individuality and performs miracles; he is presented as one representative of the divine will. Finally, the attachment of the disciples to Christ's individuality, to his external presence in a here and now, is the very source of the transformation of Christianity into a positive religion. Therefore Hegel can say: "A religion was not originally positive, it could only became so. Then it remains only as a heritage of the past."[12]

But we still find an essential text that shows us at what point Hegel became conscious of the connection between historicity and of the life of man. "In a religion actions, persons, and recollections can pass as sacred. Reason demonstrates contingency in all that. It demands that what is sacred be eternal and imperishable. But by so doing it has not shown the positivity of these religious things, for man can relate to contingence and ought to relate the imperishable and the sacred to a contingent. In his thought of the eternal he relates the eternal to the contingency of his thought."[13] This last sentence in particular shows us the connection made by Hegel between reason and history. A new conception of freedom, not purely negative as in Kant, ought therefore to be made manifest. It is a question of a living freedom, of a reconciliation of man with his history. It is more possible that this history is presented to him as foreign, in which case we will speak of positivity, of an external relation between man and the absolute. Such is the destiny of the unfortunate peoples of history; but in the other cases there is no breach between man and his history. It is only an abstract and judgmental reason that speaks wrongly of positivity.

Therefore, the relation between this historical element and reason is the cause of it. By the very idea of life, by the idea of concrete man as opposed to the abstract concepts of the eighteenth century, Hegel is elevated to a more profound conception of freedom. But this conception, the key to his future system, can only receive all its meaning if one considers the other fundamental concept from Hegel's youthful works, that which reveals the tragic in his vision of the world, namely, the concept of Destiny.

2. The Idea of Destiny

With the idea of destiny (destiny of a people, destiny of an individual, and destiny in general), more than with the idea of positivity, we are at the heart of the Hegelian vision of the world. We have been able to maintain that this is a certain conception of the tragic, which is at the foundation of the Hegelian dialectic and which, before receiving its logical consecration by a theory of negativity and contradiction, inspires the first Hegelian meditations on history.[14] Although the term destiny, and in particular the expression of the destiny of the Jewish people, is already found in the Berne works, especially during the Frankfurt period, that notion, so inspired by Hellenism and the Greek tragedians, plays a central role in his philosophy.

According to certain commentators, the Frankfurt years (1797–1800) may mark a division in Hegelian thought. According to Dilthey, the first interpreter of the youthful works, Hegel had adopted a certain mystical pantheism during this period. Thus he had rejoined his friend Hölderlin, whereas during the Berne period he had sought to master Kant's moral rationalism and had adopted his conception of man's moral freedom. In fact, our previous study on positivity has certainly shown us the passage from an abstract reason, from a continuing negative freedom, to a new concrete and living reason.[15] Positivity was the irreducible fact with which pure reason clashed. But if Hegel did not wish to abandon human autonomy, neither did he wish to renounce the riches of life and the fullness of historical changes. The concept of human nature in general was too dry and too poor to be used as a measure of the tree of life. Therefore, we could not speak of an absolute division between the Berne years and the Frankfurt years. Rather, there is a continuity of development. But it is certain that the idea of life, the idea of the profound unity of all life, and the idea of the irrational relation between our finite life and infinite life, Hölderlin's ἕν καὶ πᾶν (one and all), henceforth dominate Hegelian thought. Therefore, we could say more justly with Glockner, another interpreter of Hegel, that what occurs initially during those Frankfurt years is the irrational element in all life and all manifestation of life.[16] However, the future author of the *Logic* is not giving himself over to a mysticism and an irrational pantheism. He strives to enlarge reason in order to make it capable of apprehending this life, and the idea of destiny is precisely this rational-irrational concept that helps Hegel elaborate his own dialectic of life and history. Doubtless he will write in one of the last fragments of this era that religion alone permits "the transition from finite to infinite life,"[17] as this transition is inconceivable for reason. But his own philosophy is already an attempt to think about this transition, without yet becoming aware of that original thought, which will be dialectic. Some years later, after arriving at Jena, Hegel will say, "If reality is inconceivable, it is necessary for us to forge inconceivable concepts."[18]

But the concept of destiny is full of meaning, and it appears to overflow the analyses of reason. Even more than the idea of positivity, destiny is an irrational concept. Hegel borrows the idea from a tragic vision that, with Hölderlin and prior to Nietzsche, he sees as the somber background of Hellenic serenity.

We must distinguish, on the one hand, between destiny in general, or actual *reality*—that history of the world that will one day be for Hegel the judgment of the world *"Weltgeschichte ist Weltgericht"*[19]—and on the other hand, particular destinies that correspond to the original "pathos" of individuals and peoples. Nothing great is accomplished without passion; that is, no action or individual enterprise adequately represents the universal and the infinite. There is always in it, even if it be ample, a finitude that makes a passion of it. The destiny of an individual and the destiny of a people are the revelation of this pathos in a history. "Destiny is what man is"; it is his own life, his own pathos, but it appears strange to him.

"Destiny," Hegel profoundly writes, "is the consciousness of oneself but as an enemy."[20] By action I am therefore separated from myself and find myself opposed to myself. "Only the stone is innocent," because it does not act. But man must act. But "acting troubles the quietude of being," and whatever is not pure infinite life in us, pure coincidence with being, appears to us as if separated from us. We read in it our destiny and confront it in the very presence of life. Doubtless, in opposing and contemplating our destiny we can reconcile ourselves with it by love, an *amor fati,* which is at the same time an "I die and I become," in which man finds the highest reconciliation of himself with destiny in general and with the history of the world, which for Hegel will be the supreme consciousness of freedom. But before thinking of this reconciliation, which is the essence of the tragic, we must consider with more precision this notion of an individual destiny and what it means for Hegel.

The destiny of a religion or the destiny of a people, rather than positivity of that religion and that people, means a development in the conception of a concrete and individual totality. We know how Hegel, from the very beginning of his reflecting, was hostile to an abstract and vague cosmopolitanism. We have indicated this in speaking of his idea of *the spirit of a people,* but it is important to insist upon it again, for that view will be fundamental in his whole philosophy of history. It is, we may say, the tragic destiny of love not to be able to be extended indefinitely without losing all its depth. Love thus flees from every incarnation, every concrete form in which it solely can be mastered and realized.[21] The idea of humanity, of the "*Aufklärer,*" is an idea that, according to Hegel, cannot succeed in being realized and in uniting concrete man. "The only perceptible living unity is for Hegel, not humanity as it is for the rationalist, but the people," and history will be the dialectic of peoples, for a people is a concrete incarnation, an individual realization of spirit. It is at the same time both a totality and an individuality. This impossibility for love (and love is this living and supraindividualistic connection) of being extended indefinitely has been profoundly experienced by Christ, whose freedom to remain absolute and save the wholeness of his purity ends by being "a freedom in emptiness." "There is," Hegel says in the *Phenomenology,* "an empty extension, but there is also an empty depth." Therefore it is only in a certain form with a certain type of finitude that spirit can be realized in a particular people, and this finitude is positivity, the destiny of this people. But as there was for Hegel a positivity that was a dead remnant, and another that was a living positivity, so also this finite and concrete element, which is the pathos of a historical individuality or people, can be profoundly integrated in its spirit. It is a totality where spirit is inscribed within a particular form, as a work of art can bear in itself the infinite in the nature of a limited realization. It is therefore necessary for us to consider the spirit of a people, the spirit of a religion, or the spirit of one of these men who create history, such as Caesar or Napoleon, and who have molded their times. This spirit when it is manifest becomes their destiny, and this particular destiny, as particular, submitting to destiny in general, appears as a positivity detached from life, a remnant that ought to disappear and be transcended so that new types can be born.[22] The transition from this pantragic vision of the historical world to a panlogical conception is easy. It will be sufficient to discover in omnipotent and just destiny that involves peoples, these historical individualities, the dialectic of the idea that by its insufficiency carries in it the germ of its death. "If these moments are grasped in their purity, they are only the anxiety of ideas which are only their contraries as they are in themselves and only find their rest within the whole."[23]

In order to characterize this original spirit that becomes a destiny we will take two examples that Hegel particularly worked on during his Frankfurt years: that of the Jewish people and that of Christianity. Thus we will be able to grasp the meaning of what Hegel calls a spirit, which in history is a destiny. The very method of Hegel is difficult. It is already, by being related to things of spiritual importance, that method of "understanding"[24] that Dilthey was to apply later. To understand the spirit of a people or its destiny is not in fact to juxtapose historical peculiarities but, rather, to penetrate their meaning. Destiny is not a brute force but an inwardness that is manifested in the overt, the revelation of the vocation of the individual. Thus, it is necessary in order to apprehend the destiny of a people to effect this "original synthesis of the multiple" that Hegel borrows from Kant but applies to spiritual realities and understands in a life form: a meaning. The destiny of a people is certainly a concrete unity, the germ of which one finds in its founder. Hegel can thus write: "With Abraham, the veritable forefather of the Jews, the history of this people begins, that is, his spirit is the unity, the soul which dominates all his posterity."[25] To be sure, he adds that this spirit is manifested in various forms, according to the circumstances and the schemes of the conflicts that set the Jewish people in opposition to other peoples, but there is a unique spirit that must be understood as such and that creates the destiny of this people.

We have often referred to the story of Abraham, which Hegel has dealt with several times.[26] May we be pardoned for bringing this up again. In the

history of Abraham, Hegel believes that he discovers the distinctive characteristics of all Abraham's posterity. Abraham was born in the Chaldees, but
his first act was his separation from his family and from his people. "He
abandons his family and his native land and thus breaks the ties of love."
"The first act by which Abraham became the founder of a nation was a
separation which rent the bonds of a common life and love, all relations in
which he had lived up to that point with man and nature." This is the fine
bond of youth that he pushes away from himself.[27] He wanted to become
his own master, to be independent, to become *for-himself*, in Hegelian
terminology. But this separation from nature, much more radical than that
of other peoples, was to be the very spirit of Judaism. There is at this point a
tearing away, a rejection that could be called total, which destroys every
living relation between man and the world, between man and other men,
and consequently between man and God. This rejection or separation from
life Hegel also discovers in other peoples and other individuals who create
them, but these were not as profound. Daniel left his native land, but he did
so fighting; he carried his gods with him. But "Abraham did not want to
love." He did not carry with him the grief of those broken bonds that reveal
the persistent need for love. He remained foreign to all peoples he encountered. He did not use the land for cultivation. His spirit, Hegel tells us, was
hostile to the world and to other men. "He wandered with his herds over a
limitless land."[28] "He was therefore a foreiqner on this earth, and this
hostility toward the land entailed a hostility toward other men." "Abraham
did not want to love." What is the meaning of this essential characteristic
for Hegel? Love is what precedes every rejection and makes the unity of
life. But because of this separation from nature, by this reflection on himself
that puts an end to vital spontaneity, Abraham is no loqer able to consider
things as alive.[29] For him only those *things* exist that he needs to satisfy his
enjoyment and assure his own and his posterity's security. There is no
connection between the world and him but objective relations, relations of
reflection, but the relations of love are no longer possible. Doubtless, this
rending is an essential moment in the life of the spirit, and Hegel will say
later that "the Jewish people are outcast the most because they are the
nearest salvation."[30] And, in fact, by this rejection Abraham can no longer
consider God from a finite point of view. The real relation between finite
and infinite, which is love itself, is broken. Things are no longer anything
but things, and God is the inaccessible hereafter, which can no longer be
found in the very presence of life. Therefore, the essential character of this
spirit for Hegel seems to be, on one hand, Abraham's hostility to all vital

values such as heroism or love of human communities but, on the other hand, the discovery of what is connected to reflection, namely, intellectual values and spiritual values such as ruse, the exclusive concern with the self, and also the sublimity of an abstract universal, of an inaccessible, unique God. "The source of his God," Hegel says, "was contempt for the world. That is why he alone could be the favorite."[31] Thereby the God of Abraham is essentially different from household gods and national gods. "A family can indeed have invented divine unity, but it leaves room for other deities. It has not posited the infinite exclusively and still gives an equal right to other gods." "On the contrary, in the jealous God of Abraham and his posterity is found the demand that he be the only God, and that that nation the only one which has such a God."[32] But with this manifold separation between man and nature, man and man, and man and God, there appears what will become legalism, that is, the spirit of servitude before the letter of the law, which will become a characteristic of Judaism. God can in fact only be above, and with this separation the connection between domination and servitude is seen, which is the only conceivable one. Man is a slave, and his God is the jealous and terrible God who issues commands to man's inner life without even being present. Moses in solitude thinks about the liberation of his people. He reveals his plan to the elders, but in order for them to adopt it, it is not necessary for him to appeal to their common hatred of oppression or to an aspiration for joy and freedom. Rather he imposes external order by external means, "by miracles that Moses revealed to them and that the Egyptian magicians did as well."[33]

In this analysis of the spirit of the Jewish people, which Hegel follows from the history of Abraham to the Roman domination, we find some profound remarks on what might be called hostility between life and intelligence, or as Hegel says in his language, between life and reflection. It is this total reflection that is the spirit of the Jewish people. Life has been broken. There is nothing left but the relationships of master and slave that are conceivable among beings, for the infinite has been separated from the finite. Life is no longer immanent in living things, but the infinite is beyond and this itself becomes a thing, that is, the separated infinite. And moments of time have lost their vitality, the infinite that was in them through love, in order to become things reduced to their finitude. "The Jewish spirit," Hegel says, "had hardened the modes of nature, and the relations of life, in making things of them. However, it was not ashamed to seek after these things as being gifts from the master."[34] Thus, the desire to live had not disappeared, but it had lost its *beauty* and its grace by rejection. It solicited finite things, as finite things, and this people demanded of its God, the master, to underwrite its enjoyment of them.

It is the destiny of the Jewish people to live eternally separated from God and men so as to project its ideal outside of itself through rejection and to have cut this ideal off from life.[35]

We will persist less in the second example that Hegel gives of a spirit and a destiny, when he studied during the Frankfurt period the life of Jesus and the transformations of the Christian community. Jesus has come to reconcile his people with life through love. It is no longer a question as in his life of Jesus, written at Berne, of how to oppose morality in the Kantian sense to the legality of the Old Testament. The division goes too far, and morality is still obedience to a law, "to a master which one bears in himself."[36] The preaching of Jesus is preaching about eternal life through love, the suppression of the relationship of master and slave in all areas. He attempts to save his people, but since its salvation as a people is impossible and he clashes with the Pharisees and rulers of the people, he then addresses himself to no one but individuals: "He renounces saving his people as a people and has perceived that God is manifested only to individuals. He abandons the destiny of his people." But thereby is manifested the spirit of Christianity that correspondingly will be its destiny, the tearing away of the Christian spirit from the State. "The Kingdom of God is not of this world," "Render to Caesar what is Caesar's and to God what is God's." This tearing away will profoundly mark the modern world and will distinguish it from the ancient world. From his Tübingen works Hegel, as we have already noted, put in opposition Christianity, private religion, and the religion of a people, which was his ideal. But Christianity cannot be the religion of a people. The spiritual is henceforth cut off from the temporal, and the individual knows of a freedom that is an escape from the ways of the world. If Hegel's judgment of Christianity was severe in his first works when he opposed the wisdom of Socrates to Christian asceticism or when he noted, "Our religion wants to raise men to the rank of heavenly citizen so that their attention can always be directed above and as a result they become strangers to human feelings,"[37] he returns now to his criticism. But this criticism does not come from outside of Christianity itself, but from the destiny of its founder. In pursuing the history of the Christian community he arrives at this necessary conclusion: "It is its destiny that Church and State, service of God and service of life, piety and virtue, spiritual life and worldly life can no longer coincide." All later Hegelian philosophy that will claim to lean on Christianity will have to interpret this separation, which the student of Tübingen did not want to do, so as to try to surmount it by seeing in religion an inferior form of absolute spirit. For philosophy alone, reconciliation no longer has any bearing upon the form of an indeterminate future but is present in the actuality of the spirit of the world. The theory of forgiveness of sins and redemption is only in Christianity an anticipation of true reconciliation.[38]

Hegel deeply ponders this destiny of Christianity and discovers in it the source in Christ's attitude. "Jesus could either participate in the destiny of his people, thereby incompletely realizing his nature which was created for love, or else he could became conscious of his nature, but then unable to realize it in the world."[39] He might have been able to become integrated with his people and attempt to transform them, but then he would have had to renounce what was his true nature. He would have accepted a destiny that was foreign to him, the very destiny of his people. Jesus preferred to refuse this destiny and chose love. He had then submitted to destiny by trying to refuse every destiny, for thereby he found it necessary to be separated from the world; "Who loves his father or his mother, his son or his daughter more than me is not worthy of me." The study that Hegel makes here is the same as the one he will make about the beautiful soul in the *Phenomenology*.[40] The flight before destiny, that is, before every objective realization, is itself the greatest of destinies. Thus the Christian spirit is the contrary of the Jewish spirit. "The Jewish spirit had transformed the modes of life and relations of life into objective realities. It was not ashamed to seek after these realities as gifts from the master. The Christian spirit likewise saw in every living relation objective realities, but since, for it, as the sentiment of love, objectivity was the great enemy, then it remained as poor as the Jewish spirit, but it disdained wealth because the Jewish spirit served it."[41] The Jewish spirit had reduced the whole living atmosphere to things. It had rent the beautiful bond that united man to his universe. The Christian spirit also knows the finite character of things of the world, and it bears the infinite in its heart. But while the Jewish spirit still serves the world, the Christian spirit attempts to be separated from it, to find its freedom in the sole purity of its heart. "The Kingdom of God is in you." Thus Christ is separated from his people, whose pharisaism he knows. He is separated from the State, which he knows, however, as another power, a worldly power. "He is separated from every destiny." This is precisely his destiny, and the most tragic destiny. Hegel goes on to think about the life and death of Christ by utilizing the tragic concepts of Hellenism.

This tragic vision of the world Christianity cannot escape from, because by fleeing from all the finite modes of life, it is condemned to a separation thereby recognizing what is other, what is different. This theme is particularly developed by Hegel at the end of this Frankfurt period. This pantragicism is already reducible to a certain logical form. Every choice is exclusion and every particular affirmation is a destiny, because it carries in it a negation. And even the refusal of every particularity or every destiny is still a destiny since it results in the most radical division between the reality of the world and freedom. But this dialectic, simultaneously a dialectic of possible reconciliation, is found already set forth in the portrait of the beautiful soul. In presenting this analysis we will better understand the meaning of Hegelian pantragicism in this era.

Man is engaged in the world and has the profound feeling of his right. But if his right is not respected, he is obliged either to struggle to make it known or be resigned and submit to the violence of the world without reaction. In both cases man submits to a destiny and is placed in a contradiction. If he contends for his right, he will not recognize his right as a universal. He engages his right in reality and thereby risks it. He can be defeated. Again, in the combat which ensues he knows the right of the other person whom he faces. The conflict, which sets individuals in opposition and which is war between peoples, is the tragic conflict par excellence. This conflict is not that of right and nonright, or, as we sometimes say, of passion and right.[42] This conflict brings into opposition two rights and two passions. Thence is the tragic aspect of human existence and the history of peoples. But if man refuses to fight to affirm his right, if he resigns himself and submits passively to the violence of the world, then there is also a contradiction between this very passivity and affirmation of right. The contradiction is between the concept of right that is worthy and reality. To renounce contending for his right is basically not to recognize the reality of right. To believe in right without realizing it is the greatest of contradictions.[43]

The beautiful soul, or Christ, for Hegel at Frankfurt is the synthesis of these two attitudes, the truth of this opposition, namely, that of courage and passivity. "It is a living and free elevation above both the loss of right and the loss of combat." Concerning the first attitude, courage, the beautiful soul keeps its vitality, but this vitality retreats into itself. It locks up its right within the inwardness of its soul and removes it from all relations to the world. "In order not to see what is one's own in the context of a strange power, it no longer calls it its own."[44] In other words, the beautiful soul is not passive, lax consciousness, which still claims its right in things of the world yet shows itself, however, incapable of upholding it. It remains a living, active consciousness, but it also refuses to recognize right anywhere except in the inwardness of the soul. It therefore flees from the world in order to separate radically the *pure and the impure.*[45]

But the beautiful soul itself, which refuses every destiny, that is, every engagement in the world, submits as we have seen to the most tragic of destinies. In this separation it discovers its destiny and cannot succeed in being reconciled. However, Christ, whose "innocence is not incompatible with the greatest sin," recognizes his own destiny in this opposition to the world that has become foreign to him and surmounts it by love (*amor fati*, reconciliation of man and his destiny by love). Such is the philosophic truth that Hegel will make out of Christianity and that expresses, in a figure borrowed from the imagination, the resurrection of Christ, his victory over death, the *aufhebung* and the forgiveness of sins, the unity of the universal and particular, as the dialectic of the *Phenomenology* will show.[46]

Hegel's First Philosophy of Right

The Article on Natural Law of Jena

1. Hegel's General Position: Critique of Dogmatic Empiricism[1]

Following the years of tutorship at Berne and Frankfurt, Hegel was professor at Jena from 1801–1807. There he elaborated a complete system of philosophy that fortunately we possess in the form of his course notes. A few years ago J. Hoffmeister published under the title of *Realphilosophie* the philosophy of nature and the philosophy of spirit that Hegel created during the Jena years and that immediately precedes the *Phenomenology of Spirit*.[2] We had already known about a first logic and metaphysic, so now we are in position to follow all of Hegel's philosophical development year by year. The problem that preoccupies us here is more restricted, namely, just the philosophy of spirit and, more specially, Hegel's political philosophy. How does his youthful ideal, the spirit of a people (or *Volksgeist*) and the religion of a people, develop during these years that are devoted to the first intuitions of reflection? In order to resolve this problem we will utilize the article on natural right, Hegel's first philosophy of right, which he published in the journal edited in collaboration with Schelling, a journal that would express their common philosophical ideal. This article, contemporaneous with a system of the ethical realm (*System der Sittlichkeit*) that was not published by Hegel and remains unfinished, is one of the most remarkable works Hegel has written, remarkable as much by virtue of its originality as its completeness of thought.[3] In it the ideal of youth is expressed for the first time in a developed form, and his thought about right appears in its full originality. In fact, for the first time Hegel contrasts with incomparable clearness and precision his organic conception of right with the conception of *egalitarian* and *universal natural right,* which had been the conception of the eighteenth century and which had been expressed with unequalled philosophic depth by a Kant and a Fichte. This contrast, as has been said, full of consequences, is not only on the theoretical but also on the practical plane. The school of historical right, so opposed to the rationalistic concept of natural right, could claim this work as a forerunner.[4] In each case the division is very clear between theories of natural right (monarchist or liberal), which had prevailed up to that time with nearly every political thinker, and the organic conception of right that Hegel puts forward, whose sources are unquestionably found in the Romantic movement, which we must be pardoned from developing prior to embarking upon the details of Hegel's account.

The idea of natural secular right, which could possibly be connected to the idea of Christian right, manifested itself in the eighteenth century in two principal forms. It served either to reduce the absolutist concept of power by making the enlightened despot a servant of the State by making him aware of his obligations toward his subjects, or to found a State upon popular sovereignty by reclaiming the rights of the subjects. This latter conception is that of individualism, which had already triumphed in England, being connected to the Calvinist tradition, and in France anticipating the French Revolution, whose declaration of the rights of man and citizen is, so to speak, its manifesto. It was carried into Germany in the form of philosophic individualism in the doctrines of Kant and Fichte.[5] Thus a moral *a priori* establishes the doctrine of natural right. Universal reason is the common element, and the right of the person is the absolute right from which every theory of right should be constituted. Only the coexistence of persons necessitates a restraint to give respect to the individual freedoms of all. The State does not have any providential mission but is only present to guarantee the freedom of its members. The State is thus created for the individuals who make it up and create it. The idea of the democratic State as a servant of the development of individual abilities will be derived from this notion.

Against this rational, universal, egalitarian right, and this humanitarianism, Hegel, by relying on romantic conceptions, is going to place in opposition the idea of organic right, which reconciles Kant's and Fichte's moral *a priorism* to the positive realities of history, whose meaning we have already made clear in the first Hegelian works. The source of his thought is in the idea of the romantic life, the importance of which we have seen in the

Frankfurt period. But like Hölderlin, Hegel is going to look for antecedents in Hellenism, a Hellenism that will also be Nietzsche's and that haunts German thought in the nineteenth century. Hegel inquires in Plato and Aristotle for a conception of the organic State, the idea of a priority of nature of the whole over its parts and of an immanence of the whole in its parts. The first break with the rationalistic conception of the eighteenth century appears in the idea that absolute morality only resides and can only reside in the nation.[6] The creative energy of God is only manifested by national geniuses and by completely original civilizations that succeed each other in history. Then single and universal right is broken up. From then on right is no longer just the expression of a certain organic totality. Eternal right is no longer an abstract *a priori* that is opposed to the concrete peoples of history. Right itself enters into the field of contingent realities. It has been deservedly said that the egalitarian and universal idea of natural right is connected in occidental thought with a mechanistic and mathematical conception of science. It is, on the contrary, the idea of life and organism that Romanticism and Hegel's conception of organic right inspire. An inexhaustively creative activity is at the source of reality. It ceaselessly creates and engulfs various incarnations of absolute life. Each of these realizations is a people, and right only expresses the living realization that exists in ethical unities. It is no longer a question of realizing an abstract egalitarianism, but of thinking about the relation of parts to the whole, of members to the group, without this relation being a mechanical relation, a relation of abstract dependence, but so that it is a harmony. The idea of beautiful totality, *schöne Totalität,* is the model of the Hegelian conception of the State, which he opposes to the utilitarian or individualistic conception of the State.

Let us certainly note that Hegel does not renounce thereby a certain universalism, the idea of humanity that he had found in a Lessing, for example. He substitutes, as Brunetière would say, the universalism of agreement for the universalism of abstraction. He spurns an empiricism that would be pure historical relativism, toward which later historians will often be inclined. Each people expresses in its way humanity and the universal. As Leibniz's monads express the entire universe in a particular way, so also we ought to find in each people an organic realization of absolute right. Essence and manifestation (phenomenon, *Erscheinung*) are not isolated from each other in Hegelian philosophy,[7] but the essence of essence is to appear, and the essence of manifestation is to manifest essence. To grasp one in the other or to grasp absolute life in the multiplicity of living forms, life being completely in each of them, is the purpose of this philosophy, of which Leibniz in certain ways can be considered a forerunner.

The idea of a living organization that harmoniously rules human relations and makes the State into a true totality is a profound idea that would dominate the nineteenth century. It would be found again in various books of French philosophers who set critical periods of history in opposition to organic periods. They investigate a new constructive theory of the State after the Revolution.[8] Another consequence of the Hegelian theory of right that we are going to study is seen as related to his theory of progress. The *Aufklärung* envisaged a unilateral progress, a march toward the unity of a humanity always the same as itself, but at the same time captive of the prejudices of childhood. But the idea can no longer be true of theoreticians such as Herder and Hegel, who divide divine unicity and in peoples see realizations that are diverse but always expressions of absolute life. "A kind of pluralistic pantheism has taken the place of the rationalistic monism of the Occident," and we can even say that in his first sketches of philosophy of history, Hegel thinks less about a continued progress than about various developments, about successions of realizations as incomparable in their kind as an ancient tragedy and a drama of Shakespeare.[9] However, the idea of historical evolution will have more and more of a place in the Hegelian vision of the world, and it is almost a synthesis of the conception of progress from the *Aufklärung* with the idea of a variety of expressions of the absolute that he will give at a later time in his philosophy of history. In fact, development of the idea will be substituted for life.

The article on natural right and the *System der Sittlichkeit* complete each other. The first is destined to reveal a new way of posing the problem of natural right while the second is an attempt to solve this problem by the method proposed here. The *System der Sittlichkeit*, like the Platonic republic, is the conception of ethical life from its lower forms that Hegel considers abstract, such as individual desire, possession, work and family, to those higher forms, such as the integration of the lower forms in ethical totality, by which they truly receive their meaning. What Hegel later calls subjective spirit (psychology, phenomenology) is considered there as a preliminary moment of ethical life so that absolute spirit is presented in the form of political and social community. Religion and art, which at a later point ought to be raised above the history of the world and become absolute spirit transcending objective spirit, are still in the state of vestiges. They make themselves part of this totality that is the ethical life of a people.

There, religion is religion of the people. There is nothing higher than the people except possibly the history of peoples.

The article on natural right, which can be considered as a republic in Fichte's *Naturrecht*, thus elaborates this new conception of right in which right is an organic whole. There is no universal right that could transcend the ethical organism. Hegel ought to have placed his method in opposition to that of his predecessors and taken a position regarding the two possible ways of empiricism and abstract rationalism, which he calls the method of absolute reflection. On one hand, conceptions of natural right are found in philosophers of the seventeenth and eighteenth centuries such as Hobbes, Spinoza, and Locke. On the other hand, there is the moral idealism of Kant and Fichte.

The first two parts of the article on natural right are devoted to an appreciation of these two different conceptions.[10] Hegel, following his customary procedure, does justice to both. He analyses them in order to transcend and integrate them to his own point of view. The third part of the article is devoted to the original spirit of Hegel's moral philosophy and concludes with some profound remarks on tragedy and comedy, their meaning for human life and for philosophy of history.[11] In a last part Hegel shows the relation that can exist between the theory of natural right and what may be called positive right, between its general conception of ethical totality and history.[12] Most comparisons which our philosopher uses are borrowed from life. Doubtless the idea of life already played a principal role in Hegel's meditations at Frankfurt, but one can say that Schelling's philosophy of nature into which Hegel has just been initiated at Jena only reinforces this tendency. Hegel has not yet succeeded in translating his thought into a language that is suitable to him, namely, the language of spirit. If he already affirms in this article that "spirit is higher than nature," because nature is idea only for spirit and because spirit alone is capable of being reflected, he still appears to be Schelling's disciple on many of the points.

Schelling's philosophy, particularly his philosophy of nature, reconciled the empirical domain with the *a priori*. While Kantian philosophy radically separated form and content, concept and intuition (in spite of the well-known affirmation that concepts without intuition are empty and intuitions without concept are blind), Schelling's philosophy of nature claims to exhibit a speculative physics. It does not only want to separate the transcendental conditions of knowing nature so that it becomes a knowledge of knowing, but also to reach the very content of knowing, that is, what

constitutes the empirical domain inaccessible to thought in critical philosophy. Philosophy of nature is simultaneously an *a priorism* and an absolute
empiricism; it is an absolute realism. However, this absolute realism is not
opposed to idealism. Nature is idea and realization of the concept. In it
spirit finds itself realized. What Schelling has accomplished for physical
nature, Hegel now accomplishes for the moral world, customs, social life
and history. In this domain it is also no longer a question of opposing, in a
manner appropriate to reflection, an irreducible given, an "empirical"
thought, to a pure thought that would remain formal. It is necessary, on the
contrary, to succeed, as Schelling has done for nature, in reconciling the *a
posteriori* and the *a priori,* empirical intuition and concept. Spirit should
recognize itself in this second nature, which is spiritual nature, the life of a
people. To understand is not to reflect and separate but, rather, to immerse
oneself in the object that one studies. It is necessary to return to the primitive meaning of the word intelligence (*intuslegere*). Hegel will later write as
follows in the preface of the *Phenomenology of Spirit:* "Scientific knowledge
demands that one abandon oneself to the life of the object, which is the
same thing as what has been presented and what expresses the inner
necessity of this object. Scientific knowledge by absorbing itself in its object
is unmindful of this view of superficial completeness, which is merely the
reflection of knowledge upon itself devoid of content."[13] This method of
intellection will be appropriately the Hegelian method. It wants to reconcile conceptual thought, which determines and abstracts, with the demands of intuition.

That is why from the beginning of his study on natural right, Hegel
recognizes the legitimacy and value of empiricism. What is at fault is not
pure empiricism (perhaps the empiricism of the man of action who seizes
the whole but is incapable of expressing it in a consistent form), but the
mixed empiricism of reflection, which is neither full empiricism nor absolute reflection of thought in itself. In profound empiricism intuition, which
is the internal sense of everything, certainly exists. "It is a blunder of reason
of being unable to translate this pure intuition into ideal form."[14] It is
presented as an intuition, but reason has shown itself incapable of "setting
it forth as an idea." It is not impossible that Hegel is thinking here of great
men of action or political geniuses who seem to act inconsistently but who
have their inner logic. On the contrary, dogmatic empiricism that is raised
to science constructs consistent theories, so to speak, but in so doing rejects
"inner intuition." What does this dogmatic empiricism really consist of? It
consists of a method of abstraction that does not apprehend content in its

totality but only separates certain aspects thereby showing itself incapable of reuniting them. A proliferation of determinations fixed by the understanding is found. The primal unity of everything has been broken, and only pieces of it remain. Do we take into consideration, for example, the family, that ethical totality, and do we want to express its essence? We are held back from dividing certain determinations, such as the procreation of children, the communality of goods, and so forth, and we want to reduce this whole thing to one of these determinations posited as essence or as a law of the family.[15] Do we still want to describe the profound connection that exists between crime and punishment? We try to describe punishment by what is only an incomplete part of it, namely, the improvement of the guilty party, the exclusion of what is obnoxious, the example of punishment to others, and so on.[16] These diverse determinations, once separated and posited for themselves, are often contradictory, so that dogmatic empiricism can only clarify *theories,* in which it makes various aspects disappear that do not agree with its point of view, arbitrarily chooses one of them, and attempts to subsume the others under it. A theory so constituted is in general coherent. It unfolds as that which follows from propositions correctly connected to each other, but such a procedure is at the cost of reality. Thence the conflict is ever renewed between pure empiricism and these theories. Pure empiricism, true to an intuition that it does not succeed in exhibiting, is shown outwardly inconsistent with this dogmatic empiricism that has fixed determinations and has given to them the immutability of the concept. "We have compared the nontruth of these propositions to scientific empiricism because it accords negative absoluteness of the concept to determinations, due to the formal unity in which it transposes them. It puts forward these propositions as absolutes, and thereby shows a domination of these adopted determinations over others that are rejected."[17] But in this following step of the theory "intuition is denied as inner totality." On the contrary, because of its inconsistency regarding these determinations, pure empiricism "suppressed the violence done to intuition," for "inconsistency at once denies the absoluteness ascribed in advance to a determination."[18]

Here is the famous contrast between practice and theory that Hegel analyzes. He has already shown that this opposition originates from the fact that practice is unable to express itself in reason and that theory is incomplete. It is not theoretical enough. All empirical determinations fixed by the understanding are basically contradictory. But empirical thought attempts to avoid this contradiction that might restore life to it, permitting it to substitute a real dialectic for a consistent, though unreal and formal, theory by utilizing contradiction as an internal mover. We have stressed this dogmatic empiricism long enough. Its mistake is to reflect upon the data of experience even though this reflection is inadequate. Hegel gives two examples of these abstract theories elaborated in the seventeenth and eighteenth centuries: that of the state of nature and that of the idea of human nature.[19] In both cases we are directed to an arbitrary point of departure that is supposed to represent primal unity. In the first case we act as the physicist who speaks of a primal chaos, an invented fiction, a state where men would be considered as independent of one another. In the second case, we set an abstract possibility in opposition to the actual reality of man in his historical manifestations, a unity of faculties, starting with those one claims restore his actual state. We separate morals as far as possible, history, culture, social life, and the State, these being considered as forms more or less contingent upon human life, and we place them in opposition to this state of nature or to this abstraction of human nature. But, in fact, we can only know human nature by its development within history, and the "determining principle for this *a priori* is none other than the *a posteriori*."[20] As the physicist in order to explain the concrete properties of bodies is led to attribute more and more properties to the atom, so also the theorist of the state of nature ought to bring into this state everything he needs to explain the social state, for example, a "tendency to sociability" in man. But if in the final analysis these explanations by the state of nature or by human nature remain formal and empty, they lead to a serious opposition between original unity (conceived as a state of nature or human nature) and final unity (conceived as a social state or the historical reality of man). This last unity is none other than the State and its historical forms, but it can only result in an artificial explanation. The State or majesty, says Hegel, appears to be added externally to the state of nature. "One posits a formless harmony and an external unity in the name of society and State. The whole thing appears (in relation to the so-called primal state) to be something other and foreign."[21] In brief, the State is opposed to nature. But this opposition is exactly what Hegel wants to transcend by showing a true spiritual organism in the whole social sphere, reconciling the particularity of nature with the universality of the spirit.[22]

But Hegel's criticism bears not only on this scientific empiricism which isolates determinations and always results more or less from the opposition between the state of nature and the State. It bears above all on Kantian and Fichtian idealism, which by carrying reflection to its extreme, succeeds in separating the universal from every empirical determination. This idealism rightly conceives of the absolute, which empiricism has not succeeded in grasping because it always combined reflection with the empirical element. But it does not conceive it as a purely negative absolute in its opposition to empiricism or positivity. Freedom so attained will only be the freedom of pure reflection, incapable of being realized any other way than by the negation of every determination.

2. Critique of the Practical Philosophy of Kantian and Fichtian Idealism

Hegel wants to consider the life of the spirit or ethical life as the life of a people, and he finds it suitable here to take this expression "life of the spirit" literally. We ourselves have insisted on this importance of the idea of life and the equivalence, made by Hegel at Jena, between life and infinity. "The omnipresence of the simple in external multiplicity is a mystery to the understanding," but this nonseparation of whole and parts, this living presence of the one in the many, constitutes infinity. The concepts of life and infinity are equivalents. In the *Logic* of Jena, Hegel thinks of infinity as a dialectical relation of the one and the many, but we can recognize in this logical dialectic the very idea of life. Reciprocally, life is this dialectic itself, and life forces the spirit to think dialectically.[23] At the moment of embarking upon Kant's and Fichte's philosophies and setting them in opposition to the empirical philosophies that he has just studied, Hegel insists on infinity or the absolute concept. "Infinity," he says, "is the principle of movement and change."[24] Every determination is in fact as contradictory as it is finite. "The determined as such has no other essence than this absolute concern of not being what it is."[25] In other words, infinity is the depths of the finite; it is the principle of its development and its life. But the purpose of the Romantics, such as Schelling and Hegel, is to think about the infinite in the finite, unity in multiplicity, the absolute in its manifestations.

The importance of the idealistic philosophies of Kant and Fichte is to have posited this identity, but their essential shortcoming is that they did not succeed in realizing this except in a practical way. Fichte, who has rethought all Kantian philosophy, beginning with the *primacy of practical reason*, has certainly perceived that intellectual intuition was the identity of the Self with itself, its absolute unity and infinity. But he had separated this unity of empirical multiplicity, or positivity, we could say, employing pre-Hegelian language. As a result unity to him is only an ideal which ought to be, a *sollen*, and that ideal is set in opposition to exactly what is, to the separation of the one and the many, of the infinite and the finite. More concretely we can say that "the world is what it ought not to be so that we can make it what it ought to be." However, this demand is forever without completion or presence. The infinite is not regained in the finite but is opposed to it and is only its negation. In Kantian philosophy the phenomenon is always only phenomenon. It is empirical finitude, and the critique of pure reason does not give us the right to take this phenomenon to be the absolute but prevents us at the same time from realizing the absolute in any way at all. Fichte unquestionably made the thinking and willing subject in itself the noumenal, but at the same time he placed it in opposition to the empirical subject, and this opposition is posited by the practical self as final. We can see in this very schematic summary the two attitudes that Hegel characterizes here, namely, empiricism and abstract idealism. In the first case, the spirit isolates finite determinations and only develops a multitude of positive laws and particular principles. It is attached to positivity as such without being able to apprehend life in it, since the determinations that it thinks of are rigid and isolated.[26] Let us imagine the historian, the sociologist, or even the theoretician who extracts positive facts from social experience and collects them more or less arbitrarily without identifying them with the thinking and willing subject. These facts or determinations always appeared outside of the self so that one only reaches an empirical necessity and not a philosophy of freedom. On the contrary, "the importance of Kantian and Fichtian philosophy is that it grasped as a starting point the principle in which the essence of right and duty and the essence of the thinking and willing subject are absolutely identical."[27] Thereby these philosophies are certainly philosophies of *Freedom*. Natural right then means rational right, and it is justifiable that these philosophies be called *idealisms*. They seek to deduce laws of right and obligation from the essence of the absolutely free subject. Kant's notion of autonomy and Fichte's notion of the practical self give the highest expression of these doctrines. However, Hegel criticizes this idealism as he had criticized earlier empiricism. He only sees in this idealism a philosophy of reflection, which has been incapable of going beyond its own opposition to reflection and which consequently succeeds only in a formal identity or a negative conception of freedom.

While reading Hegel we often feel that he is only an abstract philosopher playing with concepts and juggling words. However, this is not at all true. We want now to demonstrate the meaning of that concept of reflection by which he describes the philosophies of which we have just spoken.

In order to understand him well it seems necessary to us to leave the commonplace meaning of the word *reflection*. Reflection is a sort of interpretation of life in its spontaneity. Hamlet reflects instead of acting, and action becomes almost impossible for him. In reflection we separate, by a sort of return of the subject into itself, what is united in real development, what is immediate coincidence. Let us note, moreover, that action is only possible if we assume this coincidence of the self with itself, realized in one moment or another. There is, Hegel says, in every true moral action a certain necessary immediacy. In the works of Hegel's youth we analyzed Abraham's reflection, which was a departure from the mood of his former life.[28] But in the philosophies of reflection, in the critical idealism of a Kant or in the moral idealism of a Fichte, the same thing is effected in a systematic way and the correct opposition to reflection can no longer be surmounted. Instead of being only one aspect, which Hegel does not question and especially does not question its necessity, it becomes the essential point of view. Thereby freedom, which these philosophers were correct in abandoning, is only an ideal in their system, and does not in fact exist. Otherwise expressed, it is only a negation of finished determination, of the positivity that it leaves outside itself as a denial. But this "outside," this outwardness, is exactly contradictory to the freedom for which there is no absolute outwardness.

Let us again speak more simply that these philosophers of reflection have separated the infinite from the finite and have made their unity inconceivable. If dogmatic empiricism remained a "mixture," blending an unfinished reflection with an incomplete empiricism, the idealistic systems that we consider now are dualisms. But these dualisms do not set one determination in opposition to another, such as a conception of propriety to a conception of the community of property. They put the impure in opposition to the pure, determination to the absolutely undetermined or abstract infinity. That is why, according to Hegel, they have such an importance in the history of culture. It is in reflecting on such a reflection that we can only go beyond reflection, become aware of the abstract and purely negative character of this infinite freedom and by returning to a dialectical unity that is life itself, the presence of the infinite in the finite, without being the arbitrary mixture of empiricism.

In common life we often sense an opposition between sensibility and reason. It is this opposition that the idealistic philosophies of Kant and Fichte have raised to the absolute by determining the two limits, so to speak. On the one hand, there is nature, our nature that consists of various tendencies and aspirations that we find in ourselves because we are beings of the world. On the other hand, there is pure reason, the movement of infinite unity, and freedom may consist in limiting and dominating nature within us. But even if this empirical statement corresponds to a real experience, it may not be able to express all ethics: "It would not be a question here," says Hegel, "of denying this point of view. It corresponds to a relative identity (that is, to a difference) of the reality of the infinite in the finite."[29] It is important to show that this point of view is only partial, and that, on the side of the relative identity (or difference) of the two moments, we also find their realized unity. This unity ought to produce the system of ethics. In other words, the philosophers of reflection remained, so to speak, at the moment of immorality, consequently the negative character of their Freedom, which demands that they go beyond this moment, but a demand condemned to remain without reality. But Hegel wishes, on the contrary, in thinking about all ethical life and its organization, to go beyond the stage of opposition and to show us the ethical world, which is both in its infinity and in its reality as a nature incarnating the spirit, a spirit become objective.[30] However, the opposition will not disappear so that this unity becomes a static lifeless unity. It will be what causes the development of peoples and ethical worlds, *the history of the spirit of the world.*

By remaining in abstract opposition, the idealistic philosophies of Kant and Fichte are thus condemned to be individualistic philosophies. For the point of view of the opposition of reason and nature is basically the point of view of the separated individual, while, on the contrary, actualized unity is a point of view that goes beyond the individual as such, and can only be given, according to Hegel, in that ethical totality that is a people in the wholeness of its life. "It is in a free people that reason is realized."[31]

Hegel makes his criticism of Kant and Fichte more precise by two examples that he examines with his usual accuracy and profusion of details. He analyzes, on the one hand, the abstract universalism of Kantian morality to show the emptiness of it, and, on the other hand, Fichte's system of obligation to show its internal contradiction. These two examples are particularly interesting, the first because it is a criticism of the abstract universal, beginning, according to Hegel, in its analysis of the idea of positivity, the second because it helps us to understand what will become Hegel's political realism and his opposition to the real State, which is at the same time a realization of reason "in the utopian State" that "makers of constitutions" can construct.

We have already seen Hegel attack the idea of *"human nature,"* which has been so badly elaborated. But Kantian Universalism is still poorer. It abolishes every concrete or partially abstract determination and only allows a tautology to remain, a formal identity. Thereby it too is condemned not to understand that there is a development of consciousness and of things elaborated more or less by the spirit and of representations more or less full of the universal.[32] It indeed attains universality, but at the price of the loss of all reality. The "pure will" of which Kant speaks is surely pure, but it is absolutely undetermined and one cannot draw anything from it. It is true that Kant claims to give it a content, but, according to Hegel, a paralogism is there: "One ought to be able to erect the maxim of action in universal law." But, Hegel says, universality is purely formal here. It is applied to one determination as well as to a contrary determination, and therefore the principle of morality is also the principle of immorality. "It is only a blunder, an incompetence of reason" if one can show it incapable of justifying by this principle any determination and therefore any action at all.[33]

Let us therefore consider Kant's very example: a deposit that has been entrusted to me. I want to know if I should return it (and by raising the question, by reflecting on the immediacy of my action, I am already on the path of immorality). If I do not restore it, I certainly destroy the idea of deposit or (in order to express things in a more general way) the idea of property. The determination of property thus gives me the following tautology: "Property is property, and property of another is property of another." But Hegel asks, what contradiction would exist if there were no property at all? We also might indeed say: "non-property is non-property." If we now want to know if property ought to be, it is unnecessary to remain in this abstract determination. Property only has some meaning in a historical and human continuum. Kant's error is therefore twofold; it isolates, as the empiricist does, one determination (here property) of the whole to which it belongs from the context that gives it meaning. It gives to it a form that suits everything and hence justifies anything. Therefore, Kant wrongly believed he had found the content of obligation in its form. In fact, the idea of *pure will*, opposed to every determination, only remains for us in the Kantian system as a formalism, which is given positively, but which, according to the essence of infinity (that of always being its own contrary), is only an absolute negation of all positivity. Kant's failure is not, moreover, the very failure of his age in the pursuit of a universal legislation applicable in every time and place.[34] In so doing, this age fails to recognize the true idea of the spirit, which is always concrete and living, always developing but not losing its infinity, and which Hegel proposes for consideration.[35] Kantian philosophy fails to recognize the spirit; it only knows the abstraction of the spirit's infinity.

The second example is that of Fichte's system of right, cited by Hegel as being the most consistent that this idealism has been able to reach. In it opposition, which is, as we know, the ultimate point of view of this system, appears as *legality* and *morality,* as a doctrine of right and a doctrine of morality, (*Naturrecht* and *Sittenlehre*). Fichte had abandoned the identity of the thinking and willing subject and abandoned the principle of obligation and right, the essential thesis that expresses the very idea of freedom. But as the aim of these philosophies of reflection is to determine an opposition and not to be able to go beyond it, Fichte's philosophy ought to state the nonidentity of the concrete subject and of this universal principle. Expressing this in a common way, we can say with Fichte that "trust and fidelity are lost." Men do not act immediately on the principle of right and obligation, and consequently there is a separation between universal will (Rousseau's general will) and individual will. This separation involves the organism in a system of *restraint* that is expressed in the world of right and in Fichte's theory of the State and that even extends to the organization of a police State, which Hegel finds ironic.[36] In opposition to this equality through restraint, Fichte conceives a morality that might express the identity of the thinking subject and universal law. But this identity is completely relative since it is opposed to legality. The separation of legality and morality, one completely external, the other completely internal, results in a dualism in which both terms are irreconcilable, although they only have meaning for each other.[37]

Again Hegel will want to go beyond this opposition in his own system of right. The external (legality) and the internal (morality) will be reconciled in the concrete life of a people, and the real science of the spirit will be rather that of objective right, while what Fichte called morality will only be the partial and negative viewpoint of the individual. Individual morality will only express the inferior point of view of the individual regarding the ethical world, the world of morals of a people where morality and legality are completely united.

We have said that Hegel's example was interesting here because it aided us in understanding his political realism. In fact, in studying Fichte's system of right, he is led to present some very pertinent concrete criticisms. Since in this system confidence between men is lost, it is necessary, as a famous saying states, to force the individual to be free,[38] and so to realize the general will despite possible human resistance. But the difficulty arises at this point. The general will ought to take form. But every incarnation of this general will is illusory. Since Fichte starts from the separation of the general will and the particular will, we do not readily see how they can ever be rejoined. He formulates a constitution that ought to exhibit the realization of this general will but is only an inapplicable system. Those who govern do not necessarily express the general will, but those governed do not express it either. Therefore it will be necessary that each limit the other. This is a problem of balance, but we see that working this out means there can only be a sort of perpetual movement, a mutual action of the foundation upon the top of the pyramid of State and the top upon the foundation. But this *perpetuum mobile* would be in the final analysis only a *perpetuum quietum*. Action becomes impossible in the State, for it would break the equilibrium, and even the ephorate praised by Fichte may not be able to resolve this problem.[39] It follows that action is necessary and breaks the arbitrary constructions of a utopian State. Have we not seen a recent example in a neighboring country, says Hegel, who is certainly thinking of Napoleon.

Thus it is not a question of constructing a utopia, a model of the State that may be only more or less a mechanism in regard to life. Hegel's purpose is different. In every real State there is already the idea of the State, and it is a question of apprehending it, as we find life in the midst of everything living. Doubtless there are some States more or less successfully developed, some more or less pure reflections of the spirit, but it is not a matter of constructing a utopia, but only of understanding the spiritual organism that is the presence of the infinite in the finite, concrete and positive manifestation of the absolute.

It is this task that Hegel now plans. The separation of the universal and the particular, which the idealistic philosophies present, will be surmounted, but the moment of reflection or infinity will always exist, for spirit is not completely realized in a single people but is the history of peoples and development. This dialectic of history already will have its place in the Jena system that we are studying at this time. But through the influence of Schelling it will be less important, it seems to us, than in Hegel's later philosophy. Intuition still prevails unduly over the concept, the fine ethical realization in which the spirit is recognized in the infinite development of history that will express Hegel's original spiritual dialectic.

3. The Ideal of the Organized Community

After refuting empiricism and abstract idealism, Hegel sets forth his own conception of natural right, right which, while retaining its infinite and ideal character, is connected to a disposition and is the right of the particular disposition that is realized in history. This ideal is that of the living and organized community, the fine ethical totality that the student at Tübingen traced to Greek antiquity. As his biographer, Karl Rosenkranz, rightly remarks, Hegel has later written a *Philosophy of Right and the State* and has learned how to give a more precise and systematic expression to his thought. But in this first work at Jena the originality of his conception is manifest in the purest and liveliest form.[40]

There is, however, a difficulty in the Hegelian exposition, and by failing to perceive it, one risks some danger in comprehension. In reading this article on natural right and more particularly the description that he offers of the ethical community with its social states, its military aristocracy, its bourgeoisie and its peasantry, we always wonder if it concerns an ideal or a historical reality. On the one hand, Hegel refuses to construct a rational State that would exist only in the imagination of a theoretician. On the other hand, his philosophy is not that of any particular State that has existed in history. The problem of the contact between this essential representation of the State and historical positivity is continually posited, and, in spite of the last part of the article devoted especially to the notion of "historical positivity," it is very necessary to recognize that the problem is not truly elucidated.[41]

This is due to the fact that Hegel here carries the conception that Schelling has made of the work of art over to the plane of the philosophy of the State. "The great work of art, divine in essence, is collective organization, great thought that haunts the spirit of men in all eras of social crisis." Such, it could be said, is indeed the starting point for Hegelian thought. It is therefore a matter of presenting this work of art, this idea of the State, that is present in every historical realization without causing its concrete flavor to disappear. Hegel appears to us to have become particularly aware of this problem in the following remark: "There is always a noncoincidence of absolute spirit and its expression."[42] However, in order to present this absolute expression of spirit, it is unnecessary to flee from the concrete and renounce in every expression what the advocates of a nebulous cosmopolitanism do, who lose themselves in the abstraction of a human right in general, of a State of peoples, or of a republic of the world.[43] In this case we no longer gain the community whose essence we seek, but only some formal abstractions "that are just the contrary of ethical vitality."[44] It is appropriate therefore, Hegel adds, to look for "the sublime idea of ethics, the fine form that presents it most adequately."[45] However, this aesthetic presentation of the idea of the State is insufficient by itself. Hegel certainly recognizes the concrete that embodies the right in a living people and stresses the historicity of the existence of this people, a historicity manifest by war in general. But *historical existence* is not yet history in its full sense. Under the influence of Schelling, Hegel poeticizes, if we dare say so, his conception of the State. His representation of the ethical world, in spite of profound suggestions on which we plan to insist, remains too static. Hegel's philosophy of history is still only in a sketchy state.

It was necessary to insist on this difficulty, for Hegel goes on to become more and more aware of certain irreversible evolutions from the ancient State to the modern State, and in the *Phenomenology* the place of history, properly determined and no longer merely about historicity, will be much more important than in this article on natural right. The spirit of the world in which peoples are parts will be raised clearly above the spirit of a people. Here, however, what Hegel wants to understand and present in a fitting institution is the essence of the organized community that could only exist in history as *people,* a description of an essence that cannot be the construction of a utopia. But in the very course of his presentation, he will meet the problem of a historical evolution of this community and should take account of it. The citizen of antiquity and the modern bourgeois are no longer on the same plane. Philosophy, which ought "to respect necessity" and be reconciled with it, will be unable not to record this transformation of the spirit of the world. The structure of the State will feel the consequence of it, and the modern State will no longer be able to be conceived on the model of the ancient State. Even absolute spirit will be raised above the history of peoples in order to contemplate itself in a new dimension as art, religion, and philosophy.[46]

The point of departure of the Hegelian account is this monumental affirmation. "The positive in the ethical order is this: that absolute ethical totality is none other than a people."[47] A people is therefore the sole concrete incarnation of the ethical. As we have seen, we would be unable to transcend a people without causing ethical essence to lose its vitality and without falling into unreal abstractions. But a people is an *individuality.* "That is an aspect of its reality, and considered independently of this aspect, a people would only be a creation of reason. It would be the abstraction of essence without absolute form, and this essence would thereby be justly without essence."[48] In the system of Jena, which takes a vitalistic form, absolute life only can be expressed in the individuality of peoples. A people is an ethical totality. It is a spiritual organization and thereby infinitely transcends isolated man who can only be truly realized by participating in it. But it is also an individuality and therefore has in it the moment of absolute negativity, which Hegel calls, in the text that we have just cited, absolute form in contrast to positive essence.

But individuality is oneness and exclusion. A people is unique in history; it has its own genius, a manner of existing for itself, and thereby is even opposed to other peoples. It excludes itself from other individualities.[49] Therefore, the necessity of war in the life of peoples is shown. "By the absolute identity of the infinite and the positive, ethical totalities are formed which are peoples. Peoples are therefore constituted as individuals, and as individuals they confront other individual peoples."[50] The relation of people to people can be a relation of coexistence, a more or less stable order of peace. But from the very fact of the individuality of a people, its exclusive and negative character, it is necessarily at one moment or other a relation of war. War is the great demonstration of the vitality of peoples. In war they manifest outwardly what they are inwardly and affirm their freedom or fall into slavery. It is also on the occasion of war for a people that its single individual is raised in some manner above himself and shows his unity with the group.

War appears to be explained in a people by strange circumstances. The conflict that breaks out has various causes on each occasion, and they appear more or less contingent to historians. However, the necessity of war in general is no less affirmed by Hegel. Contrary to the philosophers of the eighteenth century who had sketched projects for perpetual peace and plans for the juridical organization of humanity, Hegel, who observed the wars of revolution, develops a philosophy of history in which war plays an essential role. War for him is not the result of hatred between peoples. The single individual can certainly experience a hatred for another individual, but it is not the same with peoples,and every passion of this sort is excluded here.[51] But war that "puts in play the life of the whole" is a condition of the "ethical health of peoples." Without war and without the menace of war impinging upon them, a people risks losing its sense of freedom little by little. It habitually falls asleep and sinks into its attachment to material life. That is why Hegel does not hesitate to say that a too lengthy peace can cause a nation to be lost. Therefore "the agitation of the winds preserves the waters of the lakes from stagnating."[52]

War is therefore less an external manifestation in the life of a people than an inward necessity. Doubtless, war apparently comes from the coexistence of individual peoples, but it is inscribed in the very notion of individuality. Individuality is determined, and as such it is not free. Its freedom only appears when it denies in itself every determination and thus reunites with the universal.[53] War is a negation of negation, the real life of a people, its positive particularity exactly constituting limitations or negations. In war these negations are denied, and the highest freedom consisting of not being a slave to life comes to light. In the *Phenomenology*, in a section relevant to the ethical community, Hegel expressing the same idea will say on the subject of war: "In order not to allow particular plans to take root and become hardened in this isolation, and so in order not to allow every-thing to disintegrate and the spirit to dry up, government ought through war to disturb them in their inwardness from time to time. Through war it ought to disturb their order which occurs habitually and violate their right to independence. In the same way as in the case of individuals, who, by sinking into this order are detached from the whole and aspire to the inviolable being-for-itself and to the security of the body, the government ought, by this assertive deed, to make them sense their master, death. Because of this dissolution of the form of subsistence, the spirit curbs its being swallowed up in the natural being-there, far from the ethical being-there. It preserves the inner nature of consciousness and raises it in free-dom and in its authority."[54] Our role here is not to appraise Hegel's judg-ment on the spiritual necessity of war. We only want to insist on the heroic conception of freedom that it implies in some way upon the premises of the Hegelian philosophy of history. Let us note, in the first place, that the period in which Hegel writes and elaborates his philosophy is a period of historical importance. History is manifested in this period as the destiny of individuals and peoples. In France the tragedy of the Revolution unfolds. According to Hegel, an implacable logic leads from the Revolution to the Terror, which bears the threat of death upon individuals. It is necessary in such grave moments that the State be maintained. In Europe wars follow one another, and projects of perpetual peace appear oddly utopian. "Ger-many in short," in Hegel's expression, "is not a State in this era."[55] Centrifu-gal forces create an obstacle to its unity. It endures war on its own territory without being able to put an end to its internal dissensions. It has neither political unity, nor military unity, nor financial unity. Hegel realistically proves this by drawing the lesson from events. His philosophy aspires to be an effort to think about this history and to be reconciled with it. That is why the conception of freedom that he proposes is a heroic conception. The free man is the one who does not fear death. In contrast to this negation of nature in which Fichte's infinity of freedom consisted, Hegel gives his concrete meaning. The acute manifestation of pure freedom is death in which all that is determined, even negation, is denied on its part.[56] "This absolute as negative, pure liberty, is death in its phenomenal manifestation, and by death the subject is shown to be free and raised above all constraint." Only slaves remain because they have chosen life over liberty.[57] But the free man is he who is not a slave to life and to the vogues of existence. The fundamental ethical virtue making man free is therefore courage, and the aristocracy Hegel envisages is that of free men, both capable of thinking about the whole and of completely sacrificing their life for their people. We have already said that for Hegel war was not a hatred between peoples; neither is it simply a vital condition. It is not a question of securing its life at the expense of another people for, in this case, war would not be the manifestation of freedom. One can speak merely of a struggle and rivalry for conditions of material existence, but then the vital necessity of war would not be a spiritual necessity. If wars seem to be presented in this way in history, it is only an appearance, according to Hegel. Their true meaning is, on the contrary, domination over the natural element that always encroaches and hinders man from being raised to freedom.

A people is in fact a certain *positive nature* that Hegel calls inorganic because it is not pure life, pure liberty. And this nature is made up by the physical needs of the citizens, their work, and the possession of certain goods. The latter follows a necessity and forms a system of mutual dependence that a new science envisages, namely, "political economy." Hegel is aware of the increasingly important place of this science of social philosophy, but he insists on the necessity of its subordination. Perhaps on this point Hegelian philosophy differs the most from the Marxists who claim him. In fact, Hegel says of this world of economy: "What is negative by its nature ought to remain negative and ought not to become something set or fixed."[58] And he adds: "In order to prevent it from not being constituted for itself and becoming an independent power . . . ethical totality ought to maintain it in the expression of its negativity." It is as we have seen in large part the role of war that, as negation of negation, gives to this inorganic nature the sense of its dependence and prevents liberty from being swallowed up.

War is therefore necessary in the life of a people because without it the sense of the whole or its unity disappears and human life would collapse into a spiritless naturalness. But war also has some nefarious consequences that Hegel particularly insists on in the *Phenomenology*. This is the result of the fusion of particular national communities in an empire such as the

Roman Empire, which gathers individual peoples in a "pantheon" and makes them lose their particular unity, their original individuality. Such an empire could not be an end of history, any more than a federation of States proposing that it assure a perpetual peace.[59] Hegel, who had admired the genius of Napoleon so much with his understanding of the State, had never insisted, on the other hand, on his imperial politics. Napoleon was a collector of lands and created an empire like the Roman Empire. Hegel thinks such an accomplishment has no true significance. A necessity of spiritual life is that of particular peoples. Spirit only incarnates itself in history in this concrete form. Hegel has already insisted in his first works on the destiny of love, which cannot indefinitely extend itself without losing its depth and concrete force. In the *Phenomenology* he retraces the evolution that leads to the disappearance of ancient cities in a spiritless empire. Then the State becomes remote and hostile, and individuals retreat into themselves, which is the first form of the unhappy consciousness, as we have already noted. Private life and private right become abused, and spiritual freedom disappears.

Neither the empire nor the confederation of States can form the solution to the problem posed by the multitude of the spirits of particular peoples. History alone will form the solution to this problem in Hegel's final philosophy: "What history shows us, a series of civilizations and States appearing successively on the first plane of the historical scene, attaining their peak and sinking to reappear no longer . . . . The success of a State, its momentary preeminence, is the success of a spiritual principle that expresses the highest degree which the divine spirit penetrating the world has attained at this moment. It is then the individual who represents the universal, but represents it imperfectly. And that is the cause of its demise, which springs from an immanent justice: history is a theodicy."[60]

This vision of the history of peoples, reconciling the theory of the variety of original civilizations and that of a development, is not yet developed in the work of Jena, which we are considering at this moment. But what is found there explicitly is this philosophy of war on which we have insisted at length because it is one of the distinguishing characteristics of Hegelian thought. To this philosophy is connected the idea that Hegel makes of the social organism as it is divided by necessity into classes or individual States (*Stände*). The life of a people is an organic life; it thus presupposes in itself a diversity. This diversity is constituted by particular classes that express each in their own way the whole. Concerning the nature of these classes and their functions, Hegel will endlessly adapt his analysis to the contemporary situation.[61] In the *System der Sittlichkeit* and in the article on natural right in Jena, he will distinguish between the following: first, a military and political aristocracy, the latter alone being free because it alone thinks of the whole and is raised above the particularity of natural needs; second, an active bourgeoisie for the making of wealth and trade that confines itself to the private life, only seeks the security of possessions, and attains the whole, the universal, only in an abstract way (in right); and finally, a peasant class, having in its actual labor a certain immediate sense of the whole and participating in the universal by the basic attitude of trust. What is important in this analysis is the distinction that Hegel makes between a class of free men and one of nonfree men. Free men are those who are capable of courage in war and who live in and for their people, but the others cannot attain such a thought about the whole. They cannot revel in the concrete whole and consciously participate therein. Thereby they live in the "difference." The whole of their people still remains to them a foreign thing that they feel in the mood of fear, obedience, and confidence, or that they express in an abstract form in the universality of a right that remains an obligation.[62] Only in religion are all men equal, according to a remark that Hegel makes here and that he will develop more and more in later writings. Therefore absolute spirit will be different from objective spirit. In the French Revolution they wanted to abolish these divisions and raise all men to true liberty, making citizens of all, but that was to overlook one of the characteristics of the modern world, namely, the importance of economic life and private life. Rousseau's error was to consider the citizen sufficiently but not the property owner. Therefore, in the *Phenomenology* Hegel presents the movement that results in the revolution: "Each consciousness of the single self departs from the particular sphere that was assigned to it and no longer finds in this particular aggregate his essence and his work. It can only now be actualized in a work that is total work."[63] Such will be the profound meaning of the French Revolution: to create truly the State of reason, where the one and indivisible will of the nation is present in each one. Then there would be nothing but free men, citizens. But this work is impossible, the whole is an organism, and the difference, in the technical sense that Hegel gives the term, ought to have its place there. The result of the Revolution therefore will be merely a repair or a "freshening" of the State. New aggregates should be constituted. The irreducible opposition, which creates the tragedy of the modern State, certainly appears here to be for Hegel that of *citizen* and *bourgeois*. In his last *Philosophy of Right*, he will attempt to go beyond this opposition by conceiving at the very heart of the State a civil society that will be a moment of the whole, the moment of economic life.

Hegel's article on natural right concludes with a study on the positivity of right. The problem that he then poses on the relations of positive right and natural right is similar to the one that he posed in his youthful writings relating to religion. What is essential for him is not to oppose an abstract natural right to a concrete positive (or historical) right. Philosophy as he conceives it ought to be raised above this opposition and learn to respect "historical necessity." In fact, natural right is only realized in particular peoples who are bound to particular geographical and historical circumstances. In general, these circumstances do not constitute an obstacle in the development or freedom of people. This positivity is alive in a free people. "Particularity is assimilated and undifferentiated there."[64] The side of particularity or positivity is the inorganic nature of the ethical life but a nature that it organizes by penetrating it with its life. Therefore, one can say that a people is not only the notion of individuality but individuality itself; that is, it is a unique manifestation of the absolute. "Ethical vitality of a people consists in the fact that it affects a concrete form (*Gestalt*)—in the midst of which determination is found—but not as a positive element, in the pejorative sense of the term, but as something completely unified with universality and enlivened by it." Hegel expresses his conception again in this particularly significant text: "As totality of life is contained just as much in the nightingale as in the nature of polyps, so the spirit of the world has in each particular form its consciousness of itself. It is either more obscure or more developed, but it is always absolute, and in each people, in its morals and laws, it has its essence and has possession of itself."[65]

It is true that positivity also has a pejorative meaning. It refers to what is not fully undifferentiated, and is the dead remains in the life of a people. Indeed it happens that in its evolution a people saves some institutions and positive laws that are no longer in harmony with its living spirit. There are, like an inertia, social forms that resist necessary change. It is, we may say, the moment where memory is no longer organic, when the past instead of living reality is detached from the present and is opposed to it. Hegel had studied these crises in the development of peoples on the spot during his stay in Switzerland while considering the aristocracy of Berne, or while studying the constitution of Wurtemberg and the German state in his era. The unfortunate thing about periods of historical transformation is the fact that the new culture is still not absolutely free of the past. Positivity is then constituted by laws that are shown to be foreign to the new ethics.

These last remarks show us Hegel no longer thinking only of the historicity of the life of a people, but of historical development in all its fullness. What constitutes the propulsion of this development is the ceaseless opposition being reborn between absolute life and the particular forms that this life ought to take. There is, therefore, always a discrepancy between the spirit of a particular people and the absolute spirit that appears in it. That is why history is tragic. "Tragedy," Hegel says in the same article on natural right, "is the representation of the absolute position."[66]

We have already noted this pantragic conception of the world, which, according to Hegel, is fundamental. It is the first form of what the dialectic will be. One may be astonished to find in a study on right a commentary on Aeschylus' *Eumenides* and reflections on ancient tragedy and modern comedy. But these reflections are not digressions. They express, on the contrary, what is the most profound in our philosopher's vision of the world. Tragedy and comedy are not only aesthetic frameworks. They convey philosophical positions of consciousness. But these positions are not equivalents. Comedy is the elevation of man above all destiny. Tragedy is, on the contrary, the discovery of destiny and reconciliation with it. "The field of comedy," Hegel will say in his lectures on aesthetics, "is constituted by a world in which man as individual has erected himself as absolute sovereign of all realities that usually have worth for him as essential content of his knowledge and action, a world whose ends thus destroy themselves by their own inconsistency." Comedy expresses therefore the dissolution of all that is finite. But individual consciousness that is therefore raised above all destiny proves to be the most terrible of destinies. It grasps the awareness that God himself is dead and only succeeds in opposing the universe without truly reconciling itself with it.[67]

That is why Hegel says that "tragedy alone expresses the absolute position." The Destiny of the divine is not in fact to flee from every positive realization, but to be manifest in the finite in order to be found in it. Therefore it exists only as the tragic hero or the spirit of a people in the history of the world. Conversely, the destiny of the finite is to express the divine, to manifest in it infinite life. This twofold requirement may not be realized in a static synthesis, a noble totality that might avoid history. But the history of the world is this tragic tension, by which immanent infinite life in its manifestations demands of each of them an unceasing supersession of itself. Each expresses and does not express the absolute. That is why it dies and becomes.[68] In this reconciliation with its destiny, spirit is truly raised to freedom. Hegelian dialectic will only later on express this pantragic vision of the world in logical terms. Negativity is at the very heart of the absolute, which could not be conceived independently of it, as if it could be beyond the tragic aspect of universal history. In a celebrated text in the preface of the *Phenomenology,* Hegel will reproach Schelling for having separated the absolute from negativity: "The life of God and divine knowledge can now, if one wishes, be expressed as a play of love with itself, but this idea is reduced to edification and even to pointlessness when the serious, the painful, the patience, and the work of the negative is lacking."

V

The Modern World

State and Individual

We have tried to present the formation of Hegelian thought from the notion of the spirit of a people to the ideal of the organized community, as it is found developed in the *System der Sittlichkeit* and in the Jena article on natural right. But the Hegelian conception is still anachronistic in certain respects. The ancient city, the Platonic republic, is a direct inspiration for Hegel in his system of the ethical world. This Platonic representation of social and political life floats a little too much above history and does not take sufficient account of the distinctive characteristics of the modern mind and the State that corresponds to it. In the years following the editing of these works, Hegel will become, on the contrary, more and more aware of the difference between the ancient State and the modern State. His definitive *Philosophy of Right* will be sketched in the course of 1805–1806, which immediately precedes the *Phenomenology*. It remains for us to consider these works of Hegel on the modern State. The notion of the spirit of a people and the tragic vision of the world, which have appeared to us in the center of Hegelian thought, will not disappear, but the presentation that Hegel will make of political and social life will correspond more directly to the history of his time.[1]

We know, moreover, that Hegel had not stopped reflecting on the events of which he was spectator, such as on Napoleon, whose idea of the State he admired so profoundly, and on the wars of the empire, which were contemporary events for him. In a text of 1821 in which he sets forth his philosophy of war, we note once more the feelings experienced by him at Jena in 1807 at the time Napoleon's troops passed through: "It is true that war produces insecurity in ownerships, but this real insecurity is only change that is necessary. In pulpits there is endless talk about insecurity, the frailty and the instability of temporal things. But each one thinks, however affected he may be, that he will save what belongs to him. When this insecurity actually appears in the form of Hussars with drawn swords, and when all that ceases to be a joke, then these same enlightened and roused people who have predicted everything will begin to curse the conquerors. However, wars take place when they are necessary. Then the crops come up once again, and the gossips are quiet before the gravity of history."[2] Hegel was still saying at Jena that "the reading of newspapers was a sort of realistic morning prayer." One finds one's place in the world upon awakening, takes on its development and gets one's bearings. That is why Hegel himself could not be content with a political and social ideal that did not correspond to the history of the world, to the development of the spirit of the world in his era (*Weltgeist*).[3]

But one of the characteristics of the modern world is the development of individualism in all its forms. Since the sixteenth century individualism has become a distressing problem. Society, that is, political institutions and the State, are manifested as constraints against which man ceaselessly revolts.[4] These are dams raised against the will of the individual's power, but we must climb still higher. In Christianity and the Christian consciousness the source of this individualism is found in the principle of "absolute subjectivity." The division of consciousness into two worlds, which is expressed by the famous phrase, "Render to Caesar what is Caesar's and to God what is God's," prevents man from finding his absolute in the terrestrial City. The State is therefore only an objective reality that is opposed to the knowledge that the individual has of his absolute value in himself, and this knowledge, on the other hand, remains shut up in his subjectivity. This most tragic opposition was not found in the noble liberty of the ancient city. The ideal of Hegel's youth was, in brief, the fusion of two worlds into the religion of a people that was the consciousness of its original spirit, this objective freedom of the citizen who found his will absolutely realized in his State.

In the *Phenomenology* Hegel has considered the French Revolution as an attempt to surmount this separation into two worlds. The state should became the immediate expression of the will of each one again. "Heaven proceeded to be found transported to earth."[5] However, the Revolution failed and resulted in terror, or in anarchy, being two sides of the same phenomenon. It was Napoleon who then recast the modern State.

The identity of the will and the general will, of the individual and the

State, cannot therefore be established at once as was the case in the ancient world, but a mediation is necessary. Truly freedom for the individual is to ascend to the general will and to participate in this objective organization that transcends him. The State for Hegel is nothing artificial; it is reason on earth. But this elevation or liberation is no longer immediate. There is a conflict, latent or manifest, depending on the case, and the modern State understands the simultaneous opposition of the individual will with the general will as its reconciliation. We are going to consider some of what Hegel considers to be the distinctive characteristics of this modern State and of their relations to the individual. We will insist initially on the difference, now clearly perceived by him, between the ancient city, his ideal of youth, and the modern world. Hegel believes it his duty to deduce the necessity of modern monarchy in opposition to ancient democracy. We will afterwards see various expressions of the opposition of the individual and the State, the State manifesting itself as tyranny on one hand, and the related freedom of the individual in the economic world, or what Hegel calls civil society, on the other hand. Finally, we will show how the State, in the proper sense of the term, is above civil society and intermediary groups (such as family and corporation), the true realization of objective freedom on the earth, but how, nevertheless, there is still a world of absolute spirit above it (or parallel to it) in Art, Religion and Philosophy. In Hegel's courses on the philosophy of the spirit in 1805–1806, we will find these various points illuminated for the first time. Only the *Philosophy of Right* of 1821 and the *Encyclopedia* will give them a definitive form, by reasoning out what is presented in these courses in outline.[6]

In the *System der Sittlichkeit* and in the article on natural right, Hegel cites Aristotle and especially Plato. He would want to present a collective organization as Plato has done in his Republic. But in the course of 1805–1806 he becomes aware of the differences between the ancient ideal of the city and the modern world. "In the ancient world the fashionable public life was the custom of all . . . , it was an immediate unity of the universal and the singular . . . a work of art in which no part was separated from the whole."[7] The self only knew itself in its objective presentation, which was the city harmoniously organized by the idea of justice. Moreover, this idea was not, according to Hegel, a utopia constructed arbitrarily by a philosopher. "Plato has not set forth an ideal, but he has understood the internal principle of the State of his time."[8] In the *Philosophy of Right* Hegel says again, relevant to the platonic Republic: "Plato, in the *Republic,* sets forth substantial ethics in its ideal beauty and ideal truth. However, he could master the principle of independent particularity that will penetrate Greek social ethics in his time only by opposing his merely substantial State to it and excluding the principle of private property and family from its foundations, and *a fortiori* in its ulterior elaboration personal freedom, choice of profession, etc. This defect caused the misunderstanding of the great substantial truth of his State and caused it to be considered as a dream of abstract thought, or what an Ideal is often called. The principle of infinite personality, independent in itself of the individual, or the principle of subjective freedom, which appears inwardly in the Christian religion and outwardly (therefore connected to abstract universality) in the Roman world, does not find its rightful place in the purely substantial form of real spirit. This principle comes historically after the Greek world."[9] Now it is this principle of subjectivity (the knowledge that the individual has about the absolute in himself), which was born with Christianity and makes the modern world so different from the ancient world. The world of real life and the world of thought are different, and that is why the moral (in Kant's sense of the term) is opposed to the ethical, that is, to existing morals. "At last in religion that is no longer the religion of a particular people, each one raises himself to the intuition of himself as a universal self: his particular nature, his social class disappear as ghosts; the individual is knowledge of himself as spirit."[10]

But the platonic Republic lacks this principle of absolute subjectivity. That is why "the platonic State belongs to the past." The platonic Republic was like the Lacedaemonian State in that it was the complete dissolution of individuality. Now, on the contrary, the individual has gained inner freedom, freedom of thought or freedom of consciousness, and he sets himself in opposition to objective reality. "The spirit has been purified from immediate existence and is raised to the knowledge of itself."[11] However, it has thereby lost the very noble ethical freedom that was the unity of the inner and the outer.

This inner freedom, being opposed to the objective order of the State, transforms the State itself. Instead of an immediate unity of the particular will and the general will, instead of an expression of one through the other, an opposition is encountered at the beginning. The individual plays his part, and the State equally its part; they appear exclusive of one another. However, the State is the substance of the individual. The general will ought to be realized and reconciled with individual deviations and with the demands of a freedom that is infinite in its principle. "Deviation and disorder of the individual will must be capable of being supported; *the*

State is the ruse."[12] This note of Hegel in the course of 1805–1806 certainly shows the new conception that he makes of the State. The opposition between the particular will and the general will, between the subjective will and the objective will, is only one moment that ought to be really transcended, but that cannot take place immediately as in the ancient democracy. The State is therefore the ruse that, by leaving individuals free, comes nevertheless to be realized in the very play of their freedoms.

One important consequence that Hegel draws from this analysis is the necessity for the monarchy in the modern State and the disappearance of ancient democracy. From 1805 on, the monarchy begins to appear to him as the "constitution of developed reason." In fact, ancient democracy admirably expressed the unity of the citizen and his State. The same man who was concerned about himself and his family and worked for it also worked for the universal, taking it directly as the goal of his action. "Such was the noble felicitous freedom of the Greeks who have been so envied in our day. People are assigned citizenship, and they themselves constitute the individuality of government. They are in reciprocal action with themselves."[13] In other words, in these ancient democracies *private life* and *public life* are not truly opposed. The freedom of the private man did not exist, but rather true freedom, freedom of the citizen giving himself his laws constituting the general will, was the heart of the ancient city. Such democracy is no longer possible. Hegel will show this again in the *Phenomenology* relevant to the French Revolution.

In the modern world private man, the owner, and the bourgeois have taken on too much importance for one to be a citizen at the same time. That is why the universal and the singular are opposed in reality instead of blending harmoniously as in the ancient world. Since that time government is no longer the expression of all. It appears to have an independent existence. It is the monarch, and even the hereditary monarch, since nature plays a role in this opposition; nature is the form of this independent existence.[14] There is therefore a separation between those who govern and those governed that is characteristic of the modern State and is expressed in the monarchial constitution. But between the two extremes, the monarch and the subjects, the unity of the whole does not exist less. The modern ideal is "universality in perfect freedom and independence of individuals." The individual is free, looks after his private interest, chooses by himself his situation, and develops it for himself. On the other hand, the monarch incarnates the law and is living law, the State realized in the form of a personal will. But the unity of the whole, the universal, is saved, for this "private freedom" accorded to the individual is the force and the ruse of the State, which is lifted above private interests and dissolves them into itself. Democracy is therefore transcended, for in the modern world it would risk becoming only a complete dissolution of the State into private interests. We have indeed seen that during the French Revolution, after all intermediary bodies had disappeared, only the particular will and the general will remained present. But the domination of the particular will engendered anarchy, and sustaining the general will required the Terror.

Hegel will say in the *Encyclopedia:* "One generally is accustomed to calling a people an aggregate of private persons, but such an aggregate is the *vulgus* and not the *populus* aggregation. And in this relation the form of the State consists in preventing a people from existing and exercising power or action in this form of an aggregation. A people in this condition would be a people in frenzy, a people in whom immorality, injustice, blind and brute force rule. This would be the sea broken loose, with this difference that the sea does not destroy itself. However, such a State has often been presented as the State of true freedom."[15]

Private individuals therefore are opposed to the universal, to the State. Taken as an aggregate, as *vulgus,* a people is still without a culture. It needs to be educated and led to the awareness of the universal that manifests true freedom. It does not possess this awareness immediately but must acquire it. That is why from 1805 on Hegel criticizes Rousseau's social contract theory, or at least gives it a new meaning. The constitution of the State is described as a free agreement of particular wills. Each alienates his "natural freedom," and by this alienation the general will is formed. Only, Hegel remarks, this alienation does not occur by itself. Private man does not renounce very easily what he values, especially wrongly, as his freedom. "There is no necessity that all want the same thing."[16] One presupposes, however, that the mass of individuals has *in itself* the same general will. The general will exists therefore in itself. It is very necessary that it passes from *in-itself* to *for-itself* and becomes actual. The child in itself is reasonable, but this in-itself is at first external to him. It is manifested to him in the form of the will of his parents. Likewise, the general will appears in private men as a will that seems foreign to them. Doubtless, this is only an appearance, but this appearance is a moment of the history of all peoples that must be taken into consideration.

The alienation of nature which Rousseau speaks of is only actualized by the intermediary of a historical process that Hegel calls *culture.*[17] In the history of peoples there are moments in which the State is founded or preserved by great men who incarnate an instance of the general will and impose themselves on the people in spite of themselves: "All States have been founded by the power of great men, power not meaning physical force, for many are physically stronger than a single individual. But the great man has something in his character that makes others call him their master, and obey him involuntarily. Against their will his will is their will."[18] The role of great men is fundamental in the history of peoples because the general will needs a human instrument to be realized. The individualism of subjects makes tyranny necessary in certain eras. By this the State is saved: "This tyrannical power is necessary and just because it constitutes and preserves the State as *this* actually real individual. The State then becomes spirit certain of itself and is even raised above evil in order to reconcile evil with itself."[19]

By this last remark Hegel affirms the fact that evil is reconciled on the plane of the State.[20] What appears as evil in private life is no longer so when the issue is conserving and preserving the State. In this regard Machiavelli is justified: "His native country was trodden upon by strangers, devastated, and without independence. Each noble and each town affirmed itself as sovereign. The only way to found a State was to break up these particular sovereignties. The only way to prevail against them was by killing rebels and by the threat of death in the minds of others."[21] In like manner Hegel, by considering German anarchy, thought some years earlier that the force alone of a great man could create the unity that was in itself necessary. He foresaw Bismarck as an agent of history.

Tyranny is therefore necessary in history. But it is only one moment. Its role is to actualize this alienation of particular wills whose action is centrifugal and who avoid participating in the whole. Tyranny is a culture of obedience, but it is not imposed arbitrarily. Its justification is its historical necessity. When the general will is realized, tyranny becomes superfluous, the destiny of the tyrant disappears, and the rule of law can be exercised: "The compulsion that the tyrant exercises is the compulsion of the law in itself. But once this obedience is obtained, this law is no longer a foreign compulsion. It has become the general will known by all." Then tyranny is overthrown by the peoples "under the pretext that it is abominable and infamous, but in fact only because it has become superfluous."[22] If the tyrant was wise, he would divest himself of his power. But his rule has a violence that still belongs to nature. Thus, Robespierre preserved the State for a moment by the Terror. His force, however, abandoned him because necessity abandoned him. The tyrant is also only an individual, and his destiny is to perish when his distinctiveness is no longer reconciled with the universal, that is, when he is no longer necessary for the maintenance of the State.[23]

In the modern State a world is necessarily interposed between the individual and the State, which Hegel calls civil society (*Die bürgerliche Gesellschaft*). In the course of 1805–1806 he becomes clearly aware of the existence of this civil society, which is constituted by all private men as they are separated from the natural group, which is the family, and as they do not yet clearly have awareness of directly wanting their substantial unity, the State.[24] But already in earlier works that we have studied, Hegel has noted this opposition between the spiritual world of the State and the economic world, the world of needs and wealth. In the *Philosophy of Right* of Berlin in 1821, civil society will be more clearly characterized as one of the instances of the idea of the State in the broader sense. (The first instance is the family, the second civil society, the third the State in the restricted sense of the term, that is, the general will conscious of itself.)

Civil society (*Gesellschaft* and not *Gemeinschaft*) is none other than the state of *economic liberalism*.[25] To this State, which is the ideal for theoreticians of political economy, Hegel gives a place in his system, but a subordinated place. "If one confuses the State with civil society, and if one fixes it in the security and protection of property and personal liberty,[26] the interest of individuals as such is the supreme end for which they are gathered together, and the result is that it is optional to be a member of a State. But the State's relation to the individual is completely otherwise. If the State is *objective spirit*, then the individual himself has objectivity, truth, and morality only if he is a member of it. The association as such is itself true content and true purpose, and the destination of individuals is to lead a collective life. And their other satisfaction, their activity, and the modes of their conduct are that substantial and universal act, both as point of departure and as result."[27]

From 1805 Hegel is aware of the work of Adam Smith, *Inquiry into the Nature and Causes of the Wealth of Nations*, which Garve has just translated into German. He incorporates it into his political philosophy, but far from seeing in this economic doctrine a political philosophy that might be sufficient in itself, he sees in it rather a necessary moment, but one that reveals its own insufficiency. In this economic world man believes himself to be free. He works and possesses, has chosen his own profession, and seeks to realize his personal interest. In fact, he clashes everywhere within these limits. He remains in contingency, and instead of desiring the universal directly, he submits to it as a hard constraint that may be foreign to him. That is why on this level the State appears as the State of understanding and necessity. Civil society is a mediated realization of the universal. Its harmony, as the economists have seen, results from a kind of ruse. Each believes himself to be working for himself and even gives others the opportunity to work. What is in fact realized (the universal) and what is willed in each case (the particular) are distinct. However, from 1805, Hegel, in distinction from the earliest economists, senses the harshness of this world of wealth. He pursues these inherent contradictions and discredits it almost as a prophet.[28] The freedom that man attains in this search for his personal interest is only an empirical freedom. That is why another form of State is necessary above this world of particularity. In civil society man is trained only in the universal; he is prepared to become a citizen and to desire the universal as such.

Therefore, let us consider this economic world as Hegel envisions it. Each works for himself or his family. Division of labor allows the exchange of products, and the laws of marketing always restore a harmony at the breaking point. The visible mover of this society is individual interest, but society's inner purpose is the realization of the universal. "There is a mediation of the particular by the universal, a dialectical movement that means that each, by gaining, producing, and enjoying for his own benefit, at the same time gains and produces for the enjoyment of others."[29] This is an austere formation of natural man that is necessary in the modern world, and Hegel goes on to say, "As citizens of this State individuals are private individuals who have their own interest as their end. As this is obtained through the universal, which thus appears as a means, this end can be attained by them only if they set their knowledge, will, and action by a universal scheme and are transformed into links of the chain that forms this whole thing. Here the benefit of the idea, which is not as such explicit in the consciousness of the members of civil society, is the process that raises their natural individuality to formal freedom and to formal universality of knowledge and will, both by natural necessity and by the arbitrariness of needs, and which gives to particular subjectivity a culture."[30] In 1805 Hegel already notes this harshness of the economic world in which man is shaped. "Society has, for private man, the nature of elementary movement and is blind to what it depends on, what sustains it or suppresses it spiritually and materially."[31] By his labor and technical progress man has escaped, it seems, from the domination of nature. As Descartes would say, he has become "master and possessor," and this mastery is affirmed by the social division of labor. The content of his work goes beyond his particular need. However, if man therefore dominates nature by the power of his understanding and the common force of society, he submits to another slavery, a slavery of that very society that constitutes the universal above him. In place of domination of nature and *natural necessity*, social necessity is thus substituted: "The individual no longer accomplishes merely an abstract work."[32] Hegel now describes the contradictions of this economic world with almost as much precision as those descriptions that will be made after his time in the course of the nineteenth century.

The particular skill of the individual is the means of maintaining his existence. He can work more but thereby make the value of his work diminish. Needs are indeed multiplied and divided, taste is refined, only then man becomes a machine, "but by the abstract character of his work, man becomes more mechanical, more indifferent, less spiritual."[33] However, the machine can still be substituted for man, "as his own work becomes more conventional in this case, his work limits him to a point, and work is more perfect as it is more monotonous."[34]

Demand varies according to vogue. Some industries ought to disappear while new ones make their appearance, leaving the individual, who works at the mercy of those contingencies, blind to the movement of the whole thing. The consequence, perceived by Hegel, is the condemnation of a whole "class of men in the labor of fabrics and manufactures, a work completely indifferent, unhealthy, and without security, no longer truly making appeal to ability and personal capacities."[35] This class is afterward thrown into poverty by the incessant variations of the market.

Then the more heartrending opposition of the modern world is manifest, an opposition peculiar to civil society: that opposition of poverty and wealth. By a kind of concentration that is produced by a certain necessity, wealth increases on one hand as poverty rises on the other. "Wealth is like a crowd that attracts others to itself." "He who has, it is to him that we give." And Hegel can add: "This inequity of wealth and poverty becomes the greatest rending of the social will, inner revolt, and hatred."[36]

In the *Philosophy of Right*, Hegel will carefully note this contradiction in civil society: "If one imposed on the wealthy class the direct charge of keeping the masses reduced to misery . . . the maintenance of destitutes might be assured without being obtained by work, which might be contrary to the principle of civil society and to the individual feeling of independence and honor. If, on the contrary, their life was assured by work (the occasion of which might be procured for them), the quantity of products would increase, an excess that, with the lack of corresponding consumers who would be themselves producers, exactly constitutes evil, and it would actually increase twofold. It appears here that in spite of its excess of wealth, civil society is not so rich; that is, in its wealth it does not possess enough goods to pay financial support to excessive misery and to the common people whom it engenders."[37]

Hegel does not propose any solution to this crisis of the modern world. He only sets the picture of this civil society in opposition to the one liberalism presents. Freedom thus attained by man is not true freedom, although it may be necessary. But the State, which is "the force of the universal eye," is raised above this world. The State is its truth and it is only in the State that man is free. In the *Philosophy of Right*, Hegel envisages solely a system of corporations that, by grouping various individual interests by professions, prepare the individual for a higher task, for a more direct participation in the universal, that is, in the spirit of a people. The corporation replaces the family, which can no longer play this role in this civil society. It becomes the true intermediary between the individual and the state.[38]

This participation characterizes life for the State. Civil society ought to be transcended; it is not the true State. "The State as reality of the substantial will, a reality that it receives in the particular consciousness of the universalized self, is the rational in itself and for itself. This substantial unity is an appropriate, absolute, unchanging end in which freedom obtains its supreme value. And therefore this final end has a sovereign right with respect to individuals, whose highest obligation is to be members of the State."[39] We return here to the ideal of freedom that we have studied in Hegel's first works. The modern State is strong enough to make room within it for the division of the idea. Therefore, it contains civil society in itself; it recognizes the subjective freedom of the individual, which, since the time of Christianity, has been fundamental in the spirit of the world, and still, in reconciling itself with this freedom, realizes and posits it in reality. Hegel therefore permits the ideal equality of men, on the condition that it does not lead to a cosmopolitanism having no real historical meaning. "It pertains to culture and thought as consciousness of the individual in the form of the universal that I am conceived as a universal person, a boundary in which everyone is included as identical. Therefore, man is of value because he is man, not because he is Jew, Catholic, Protestant, German, or Italian. This awareness of the value of universal thought is of infinite importance. It only becomes an error if it is crystallized in the form of a cosmopolitanism so as to be put in opposition to the concrete life of the State."[40] That is why the State is reality in the act of concrete freedom. "The result is that neither the universal is of value and is achieved without particular interest, consciousness, and will, nor do individuals live as private persons directed exclusively to their interest without willing the universal; they have an activity conscious of this end."[41] In the phrase that follows, Hegel compresses all the synthesis that expresses the meaning of his political philosophy: "The principle of modern States has this power and this extreme depth of permitting the principle of subjectivity to be accomplished up to the extreme point of personal autonomous particularity, and at the same time of restoring to substantial unity and of maintaining this unity in this principle itself." Is this synthesis possible that may be both *liberalism* and *totalitarianism*, to use modern expressions? There is another question that goes beyond the aim of our study. We only wanted to present Hegelian philosophy objectively, and in the last part of our work to sense all the complexity and richness and all the nuances of his political thought. What cannot be denied is the importance of the Hegelian philosophy of the State for contemporary thought and life. For us French, it is essential to be familiar with Hegel's vision of the world, whatever judgment we should have about it. According to Hegel, history and reason are interpreted by each other. The formless absolute, which he grasps necessarily in history, would be "solitude without life," and history is that with which we must be reconciled. Freedom is that very reconciliation. Hegelian freedom, we have insisted, transcends the individual and his private life. It is a reconciliation of man with his destiny, and this destiny is history, which is its expression. The meditation of our philosophers on freedom is entirely different. From Descartes to Bergson, our philosophy appears to resist history. It is rather dualistic and looks for freedom in a reflection of the subject on himself. It is not that our philosophy lacks generosity in its rationalistic or mystical conception, but it would refuse to see in the State the realization of the divine on earth. It would also reject that unity of outer and inner that is expressed in the famous phase of Hegel, according to which *"Weltgeschichte ist Weltgerichte,"* the history of the world is the judgment of the world. According to Hegel himself, Christianity and the absolute value of subjectivity are slowly integrated into a system that was originally hostile to them. Absolute spirit (art, religion, and philosophy) appears to be raised above the spirit of the world that is manifested in the history of peoples. In the course of 1805–1806 and later in the *Phenomenol-*

ogy of 1807, religion is not only religion of a people; it is consciousness of the absolute, distinct from the objective development of the idea in history. Thus the church is opposed, tragically at times, to the State.[42] In Hegel's final philosophy, which desires to comprehend the reconciliation that religion only senses, one is thus led to wonder what are the relations of objective spirit and absolute spirit, the latter appearing to itself in the various forms of the world of art, religion and philosophic thought.

But this question poses the problem of the interpretation of the complete Hegelian system. It is fundamental to determine the meaning of this system in the final analysis. However, this goes beyond our task, and moreover, it is uncertain that our philosopher always presents a perfectly clear solution. There exists in his thought an ambiguity. That ambiguity is that the reconciliation of subjective spirit and objective spirit, the supreme synthesis of this system, is perhaps not completely realizable.

Notes

Introduction

1. Lucien Herr, "Hegel," in *Grande Encyclopédie* (Paris: Lamerault, 1886–1902).

2. On Hegel's years of study at Tübingen and his relations with Schelling and Hölderlin, cf. Hegel's *Tübinger Fragement* (Lund: von G. Aspelin, 1933). For Hegel's youthful works, cf. my article in the *Revue de métaphysique et de morale,* July–October, 1935: "Les Travaux de jeunesse de Hegel d'après des ouvrages récents."

3. These various works are found collected in the Lasson edition of Hegel's works: *Sämtliche Werke: Kritische Ausgabe,* ed. Georg Lasson and Johannes Hoffmeister (Leipzig: Felix Meiner, 1902–); cited hereafter as *Works*. A French translation of the article on "Foi et Savoir" (*Glauben und Wissen*) has been published by Vrin in 1952 as *Premières Publications de Hegel,* trans. M. Mery.

4. G. W. F. Hegel, *La Phénoménologie de l'esprit,* trans. Jean Hyppolite (Paris: Aubier, Editions Montaigne, 1939 [vol. 1], 1941 [vol. 2]). This was the first French translation of this book.

5. For an explanation of the moral philosophy of Fichte, a philosophy of action in which the Self and the Universe always clash, cf. *La Destination de l'Homme* (Paris: Aubier, 1942), a French translation with a preface by M. Gueroult.

6. The best explanation of the whole development of German Idealism from Kant to Hegel seems to us to be the work of Richard Kroner, *Von Kant bis Hegel,* 2 vols. (Tübingen: J. C. B. Mohr, 1921, 1924).

7. Dilthey first utilized and interpreted these youthful works. They were later collected by Herman Nohl, ed., *Hegels Theologische Jugendschriften* (Tübingen: J. C. B. Mohr, 1907); they were published in English as *On Christianity: Early*

Theological Writings, trans. T. M. Knox (New York: Harper, 1948). In France, Jean Wahl's book *Le Malheur de la conscience dans la philosophie de Hegel* (Paris: Rieder, 1929) is a particularly interesting interpretation that has renewed French interest in Hegel's philosophy.

8. To make ideas more precise, we give the following chronology of Hegel's youthful career: Tübingen, 1788–1793, Berne, 1793–1796, Frankfurt, 1797–1800, Jena, 1801–1807.

9. On Hegel and the French Revolution, cf. my article in the *Revue philosophique,* special number of September–December, 1939.

10. *Zu den Sachen selbst.*

11. Nohl, 429. Hegel adds: "The perception of pure life could be perception of what man is." Hegel's first works often cause us to think about what we have called since Kierkegaard's time existential philosophy. On Hegel and Kierkegaard, see Wahl, *L'Etude de J. Wahl dans les rapports du IIIe Congrès hégélien de Rome* (Tübingen: J. C. B. Mohr, 1934).

12. Cf. the basic work of Haering: T. Haering, *Hegel, sein Wollen und sein Werk* (Leipzig: Teubner, 1929). The second volume, which studies Hegel's development from his arrival in Jena to the publication of the *Phenomenology,* appeared in 1938.

13. In the two volumes that he has devoted to Hegelian philosophy (*Hegel,* Fr. Frommans Verlag, 1929 [vol. 1], 1940 [vol. 2]), Hermann Glockner opposes the tragic vision of the world that for Hegel is primitive to its panlogicism, which constitutes the "philosophical destiny" of it. In the course of our article this distinction inspires us to begin with the tragic vision of the world.

14. Cf. *Le Système de l'Idéalisme transcendental de Schelling,* in *Works* (1858), vol. 3; French translation by P. Grimblot, Paris. We find, however, in this work a conception of history, that is, second nature of man, reconciliation of Freedom and Necessity, which anticipates the Hegelian conception. But this is merely a suggestion.

Chapter I

1. In *Hyperion,* Hegel's friend Hölderlin represents it thus as the state of Germany in this era (in *Johann Christian Friederich, Sämtliche Werke,* ed. F. Beissner and A. Beck [Stuttgart: Kohlhammer, 1943]). The scene is really only modern Greece in revolt against Turkish domination.

2. Hegel, *System der Sittlichkeit.* In *Works,* ed. Lasson, 7: 465. Only in the life of a people does "intellectual intuition become at the same time a real intuition," "then the eyes of the spirit and the eyes of the body coincide."

3. Hegel, *Phénoménologie,* 1: 292. The spirit, supraindividualistic reality, is there defined as realized reason having become concrete being, 2: 9.

4. Hegel, *Phénoménologie.* "Virtue and the Course of the world." "Ancient Virtue had an exact and certain meaning, for it had solid content in the substance of the people," 1: 319.

5. On the opposition of *Moralität* and *Sittlichkeit,* cf. *Phénoménologie,* 1:

283. In his *Philosophy of Right* Hegel distinguishes abstract right (*objectif*), subjective morality (*Moralität*), and their unity in the state (*Sittlichkeit*).

6. This is one of the fundamental ideas of Hegelianism, the foundation of Hegel's future philosophy of history. He would not, therefore, accept Bergson's distinction between the closed and the open. For him infinity or the open must be found at the very heart of a closed society. An inadequacy certainly exists, but the result of it is only the development of history in the succession of peoples.

7. Hegel, *Works,* ed. Lasson, 7: 411.

8. One might say that Hegel proposes the problem that will haunt so many minds of the nineteenth century up to Auguste Comte, namely, how to find a religion that is better adapted to modern people than the Christian religion. However, little by little, it is philosophy that, by thinking about the essence of the Christian religion, will become its dominant preoccupation.

9. Nohl, *Hegels Theologische Jugendschriften*, 6.

10. Ibid., 3 ff., 27.

11. "In sensitive man, religion also is sensitive; the religious impulses in order to do well ought to be sensitive in order to act on sensibility," Nohl, 5.

12. "Private religion forms the morality of individual man, but the religion of a people, as well as political circumstances, forms the spirit of a people." Nohl, 27.

13. It is necessary moreover to insist strongly on this fact that in Hegel's first works the State does not yet appear restrained. The individual is free in the community that expresses him directly and free only in it.

14. Montesquieu, *Esprit des Lois: Oeuvres complètes* (Paris: André Masson, 1950–55), book I, chap. 3, "Des lois positives." Hegel praises Montesquieu for having based his work "on the intuition of individuality and the character of people." "He is not raised to the most lively idea, but at least he has not deduced particular institutions from so-called reason or has not abstracted them from experience." He has tried to grasp the individual whole, the general *spirit* of a nation. Hegel, *Works,* ed. Lasson, 7: 411.

15. Nohl, 27.

16. He does it spontaneously, without putting forward again at the beginning of these works the theory of this irreducible individuality. Hegel is always seeking to characterize in an original way individuals as they incarnate a certain spirit, such as Socrates, Christ, Abraham, Antigone.

17. Jean-Jacques Rousseau, *Du contrat social,* ed. G. Beauvalon, 5th ed. (Paris, 1938), 141.

18. Cf. also all of book II of the *Contrat social* and particularly Chap. 3; "If the general will can err." One cannot insist too much upon the influence of Rousseau on the Hegelian conception of the State. This influence has been as profound as the influence of Rousseau, though somewhat differently, on Kant and his moralism.

19. With Christianity there appears for Hegel the separation of *this*

world and the *next world.* Formerly in the ancient city the religion of a people was pure immanence. How shall we recover this immanence after having entered the Christian era of the unhappy consciousness? This appears to us in some respects one of the essential problems of Hegelianism. There would have to be a certain return to the ancient world after Christianity.

Chapter II

1. Hegel, *Leçons sur la philosophie de la religion,* trans. J. Gibelin, 5 vols. (Paris: Vrin, 1954–1959). Cf. also Hegel, *Phénoménologie,* 1: 176 ff.

2. Hegel, *Phénoménologie,* 178. "The consciousness of life, of existence, is only sorrow over this existence."

3. Hegel, *Phénoménologie,* 2: 44 ff. "The State of Right."

4. Nohl, *Hegels Theologische Jugendschriften,* 219 ff.

5. Ibid., 220.

6. Dialectic of quantitative evolution and of qualitative revolution that will find its place in the logic relevant to the category of "measure." Hegel, *Phénoménologie,* 1: 12.

7. Nohl, 220. This religion was the religion of a city that attributed its birth, development, and victories to its gods. This religion was not a flight into a hereafter.

8. Ibid., 221.

9. We know that for Hegel the philosophy of history is the history of the arrival of Freedom. But this Freedom for Hegel has a meaning that must be made explicit. The term has, for him, a metaphysical meaning that is different from the one given to it by our French philosophers.

10. Nohl, 222.

11. Ibid., 221.

12. Ibid., 222.

13. We insist further (cf. chap. V, "State and Individual") on this conception that Hegel makes of Plato's *Republic.*

14. Nohl, 223.

15. Ibid., 223.

16. Cf. what Schelling said about the State in this era: "There is no idea of the State, because the State is a machine." He expressed this thought in a letter to Hegel, which Hegel did not answer.

17. Nohl, 223.

18. The State will appear as the destiny of the individual and wealth as the destiny of the State. On this dialectic of the power of the State and of wealth, cf. Hegel, *Phénoménologie,* 2: 57 ff.

19. Nohl, 223.

20. Ibid., 224. Hegel insists here on the passivity of the Christian with regard to his God which contrasts with the terrestrial activity of the pagan. Even the martyr still shows a certain passivity in his heroism.

Chapter III

1. These various studies are contained in the volume of Nohl already cited. A French translation of the Berne *Life of Jesus* exists, translated by D. D. Rocca as *Vie de Jésus* (Paris: Gamber, 1928), and a more recent translation of *The Spirit of Christianity and Its Destiny* by J. Martin (Paris: Vrin, 1948).

2. In a very obscure passage at the end of the *Phénoménologie,* Hegel will say that the modern task is to reconcile Spirit and Time as the eighteenth century wanted to reconcile Spirit and Extension.

3. We will interpret these works on Right later. In every case, the opposition that Hegel sees relevant to the notion of positivity has a very general application.

4. Nohl, 139; cf. David Hume's *Dialogues Concerning Natural Religion* (New York: Hafner, 1948).

5. Nohl, 139. It is relevant to this positivity that Hegel for the first time thinks about the relation of "master and slave." In a positive religion man is a slave before God. He obeys commandments that are for him foreign to his will and reason.

6. There is, however, a great difference between the natural religion of the eighteenth century and *postulated* religion in Kantianism. The first depends on theoretical reason whereas the second depends on the impotence of that reason and on the demands of practical reason. It is a faith connected to moral action.

7. Nohl, 145.

8. In other words, as is often the case with Hegelian concepts, there is a double meaning of positivity: one pejorative, the other laudatory. Positivity is like memory, living and organic. It is the past always present, inorganic and separate, and it is the past that no longer has any authentic presence.

9. Nohl, 89.

10. This Berne *Life of Jesus* already makes one think of the interpretations that the extreme left-wing Hegelians will later assign to the thought of the master.

11. Nohl, 141.

12. Positivity would result, therefore, from a necessary transformation of everything that is living.

13. Nohl, 143.

14. Cf. in particular the article of P. Bertrand: "Le Sens du tragique et du destin dans la dialectique hégélienne," *Revue de métaphysique et de morale,* August 1940. The author intends to show "how in the entire system and as early as the youthful writings a certain sense of the tragic and destiny mingles in this requirement (for the absolute) and determines the meaning of it, determining thereby the form and the movement of the dialectic and thus the very development of the system."

15. Hegel's evolution, if there is evolution, in the youthful years would therefore proceed from a kind of revolutionary rationalism to a sorrowful

mysticism where reconciliation with the Universe is sought in the first place. But even in the Berne *Life of Jesus* certain mystical elements are not absent.

16. Glockner, *Hegel,* 2: 84 ff. "During the Frankfurt period Hegel attacks the irrational as he had attacked moral rationalism during the Berne period."

17. Nohl, "System-fragment." In *Hegels Theologische Jugendschriften,* 347. "The elevation of man from finite life to infinite life is religion."

18. Hegel, *The Difference between the Systems of Fichte and Schelling.* In *Works,* ed. Lasson, 1: 104–5. In this text the passage from pantragicism to panlogicism is effected. The inconceivable in the concept is the antinomy, the meeting of contradiction.

19. [Hegel, *Enzyklopädie der Philosophischen Wissenschaften im Grundrisse.* In *Works,* ed. Lasson, para. 548—translators' addition.]

20. Nohl, 283. We reflect with the author of the article cited above that "it is necessary to be immersed in these admirable pages, in which Hegel deciphers the 'spirit' of an individual, a people or a religion from the point of view of their destiny, if we wish to gain access to his method. We will have the feeling of assisting in the very birth of the dialectic." At Berne Hegel judged Christianity externally. Now he grasps it internally by its original *destiny.*

21. Love is partial or limited or it extends indefinitely. But if it extends indefinitely, then it is without profundity. This impossibility of a *concrete* love, though indefinite in extension, is doubtless the starting point of Hegel's historical thought, which is employed to determine necessarily a *variety* of notions.

22. In considering Destiny instead of positivity, Hegel is aware of introducing a living concept. *Positivity* is something objective with which reconciliation is impossible. Destiny is a manifestation of life where life itself can be recovered. "The feeling of life which recovers itself is love, and in love destiny is reconciled" (Nohl, 283).

23. Hegel, *Phénoménologie,* 2: 274. Hegel has at first conceived concrete totality as a *people,* then as *idea,* and finally as people becoming the *bearer* of the idea.

24. *Verstehen.*

25. Nohl, 243.

26. Ibid., 243, 371 ff.

27. Ibid., 245–46.

28. Ibid., 245–46.

29. Living beauty is no longer possible. The frequent use of this term "beauty" shows that Hegel never stops thinking of a comparison between the spirit of the Jewish people and the Hellenic spirit.

30. Hegel, *Phénoménologie,* 1: 281.

31. Nohl, 247. Hegel characterizes with much more precision than Herder the spirit of Judaism as it is revealed in the Bible. Herder had only insisted on an infancy of humanity.

32. Ibid., 249.

33. Ibid., 249.

34. Ibid., 230.

35. On the God of Abraham, destiny for Abraham, and the bearing of these concepts on Hegelian dialectic, cf. our article on the "Works of Hegel's Youth," *Revue de métaphysique et de morale*, July–October, 1935.

36. As we have indicated above, the opposition of morality and legalism served Hegel during his Berne period to put Christ in opposition to Judaism. Now Kantian morality is itself compared to the Jewish spirit. This morality, in fact, is not *love*. It depends upon the irreducible opposition of the *Universal* and the *Particular*, of the Law and Man. It is an opposition foreign to life.

37. Nohl, 27.

38. This is the reconciliation that philosophy ought to think about. On the relations between the Christian hope and philosophic knowledge, cf. Hegel, *Phénoménologie*, 2: 289–90. "Its reconciliation is therefore in its heart, though still divided with its consciousness, and its actuality is still broken."

39. Nohl, 328–29. "In order completely to attain consciousness of his nature as love, Jesus had to renounce the actual feeling of this in his vitality both in fact and in reality. That is why he chose the separation between his nature and the world." Nohl, 329.

40. With this difference: the study that Hegel makes of the beautiful soul in the *Phénoménologie* (2: 186) has a more critical character.

41. Nohl, 330.

42. Cf. on this point Hegel, *Phénoménologie*, 2: 31. The tragic in the Greek world is the opposition between human law, the State (Creon), and divine law, the family (Antigone).

43. Hegel himself notes the transition here, so important for his future philosophy, from the tragic to contradiction, from pantragicism to panlogicism. Nohl, 284, footnote.

44. Nohl, 286. In order to be absolutely saved, man therefore denies himself.

45. This conscious separation, Hegel says, creates the heroic vitality of Christianity: "I have not come," says Christ, "to bring peace."

46. Cf. in particular Hegel, *Phénoménologie*, 2: 198. It appears that from the *Phenomenology* on, Hegel is going to look more and more into Philosophy (which is actual thinking about reconciliation) for what in his youth he demanded from the religion of a people.

Chapter IV

1. Cf. Franz Rosenzweig, *Hegel und der Staat* (Munich and Berlin, 1920) and in French the article of Vermeil in the *Revue de métaphysique et de morale:* "La Pensée politique de Hegel" (July–September, 1931).

2. *Realphilosophie* was published in the Lasson edition, volumes 19 and 20.

3. These two works are found in volume 7 of the Lasson edition, *Schriften zur Politik und Rechtsphilosophie*.

4. However, Hegel later opposed this school.

5. On Fichte himself, there is much to say. The thought of the author of *Addresses to the German Nation* and the *Closed Commercial State* is complex in this

respect, but we will only consider it here in the form that Hegel has given to it.

6. Hegel, *Absolute Ethical Totality Is None Other Than a People*. In *Works*, ed. Lasson, 7: 371.

7. Cf. Hegel, *Logic*, *"Die Erscheinung."* In *Works*, ed. Lasson, 4: 122.

8. Cf. the ideas of Auguste Comte and Saint-Simon. But for Auguste Comte, the idea of humanity is very different from what it is for Hegel. A comparison of Hegelian and Comtian thought would be very fruitful.

9. The same is true for the history of philosophy. Before envisaging a dialectical *progress* of the Idea, Hegel begins by seeing in each particular philosophy an original manifestation of reason, a particular thought about the Absolute. Cf. in this regard the study on *The Difference between the Systems of Fichte and Schelling*.

10. See Hegel, *Natural Right*, in *Works*, volume 7 of the Lasson edition, first part on empiricism, 334–46, second part on the moral idealism of Kant and Fichte, 346–71.

11. Ibid., third part, 371–96. Our analysis will follow this very development of Hegel's thought in this work.

12. Hegel, *Natural Right*, 7: 397–416.

13. Hegel, *Phénoménologie*, 1: 47.

14. Hegel, *Natural Right*, 7: 343.

15. Ibid., 334.

16. Ibid., 335, 345.

17. Ibid., 342. In other words, dogmatic empiricism is justly what one calls an abstract theory in a pejorative sense. It abstracts from reality a particular determination and claims to explain everything by it alone.

18. Ibid., 346.

19. We have already indicated above, relevant to the idea of positivity, Hegel's attitude to this concept of "human nature."

20. Hegel, *Natural Right*, 7: 339.

21. Ibid., 342.

22. "The absolute idea of morality or the ethical order contains, on the contrary, *the identity of the state of nature and majesty*" (ibid.).

23. Jean Hyppolite, "Vie et prise de conscience de la vie dans la philosophie hégélienne d'Iena," *Revue de métaphysique et de morale*, 1937.

24. Hegel begins his account with a study of the concept of *infinity*, Hegel, *Natural Right*, 7: 347. He presents the nature of "infinity and its transformations" and places his *dialectical* conception of the infinite in opposition to that of his predecessors.

25. Hegel's first logic, developed at Jena, is actually a logic of infinity. Hegel, *Jenenser Logik*, ed. Lasson, 31. To grasp a limited determination as infinite is to grasp it in its anxiety to be transcended, in its "becoming other than itself." The error of the philosophies of reflection is in positing the infinite outside of the

finite, in this case the moral idea outside of the actual people who incarnate it.

26. Moreover, such is always for Hegel *positive science* when it is separated from *philosophy;* cf. on this point the end of the article *Natural Right*, 397 ff.

27. Hegel, *Natural Right*, 7: 361.

28. We have clearly indicated, as regards the unhappy consciousness and the destiny of the Jewish people, the existential meaning that Hegel ascribes to this reflection in which man renounces the immediate unity of life. The philosophies of reflection (Kant, Fichte, Jacobi), of which Hegel makes a study in the Jena article entitled "Faith and Knowledge" ("Glauben und Wissen," *Kritisches Journal der Philosophie* 2 [1902]) are only the philosophy of this separation.

29. Hegel, *Natural Right*, 7: 351. "The popular expression of this presentation of ethical nature as relative identity is the opposition of the real conceived as sensibility, the faculty of desiring (moment of plurality), with reason (moment of unity). Relative identity is then their noncoincidence and demand in an ought-to-be of their unification."

30. This is the origin of what Hegel will later call "objective spirit."

31. Hegel, *Phénoménologie,* 1: 292: "I intuit Them as Myself, Myself as Them. Thus in a free people reason is in truth actually realized: it is presence of the living spirit."

32. For Kant, in fact, there is a universal on one hand, the particular on the other, no synthesis being possible between them. For the Hegelian spirit, that of phenomenology, there are objects more or less elaborated by the spirit that incarnates, more or less profoundly, the universal.

33. Hegel, *Natural Right*, 7: 354. On this position of morality that becomes the dialectic of immorality, cf. also Hegel, *Phénoménologie*, 2: 176 ff.

34. Even with Winckelmann and Herder, Hegel's predecessors here, organicism is still connected to conceptions of the *Aufklärung*. It is necessary to deduce some universal *norms* from history, a canon of the Beautiful, or an eternal type of Humanity.

35. Spirit, Hegel had said at Jena, is "what is found" and thus is lost in externalization in order to give birth to itself. It is alienated and thus is saved.

36. Hegel reproaches Fichte's liberalism for ending in fact in a state of affairs where the ideal would be for the police to know what each citizen does every hour of the day. Cf. the study byHegel entitled *The Difference between the Systems of Fichte and Schelling.*

37. This is a profound thought, for, in order to separate the legal and the moral so clearly, real social life and inner morality are contrasted so that they can no longer be reconciled.

38. Cf. Rousseau, *Contrat social.*

39. Hegel, *Natural Right*, 7: 364–65, where Hegel employs his concept of irony, at times a bit clumsily, in contrast with the system of balance presented by Fichte. [The image of the ephorate refers to the system of checks and

balances in Sparta whereby magistrates had some power over the king. Trans.]

40. Karl Rosenkranz, *Georg Wilhelm Friedrich Hegels Leben,* (Berlin, 1844).

41. It will not be the same in the last *Philosophy of Right* of Hegel in 1821.

42. Hegel, *Natural Right,* 7: 415.

43. Ibid., 415–16. It is necessary to present absolute spirit in a form or a concrete figure (*Gestalt*), but cosmopolitanism is the absence of every form (*Gestaltlosigkeit*).

44. Ibid., 415–16.

45. Ibid., 416.

46. We envisage these problems particularly in the last part of our work, "The Modern World: State and Individual."

47. Hegel, *Natural Right,* 7: 371.

48. Ibid., 371.

49. Hegel confuses these two characteristics, oneness and exclusion, in his notion of individuality, which allows him to pass from pantragicism to panlogism.

50. Hegel, *Natural Right,* 7: 372.

51. This appears to be explicitly evident for Hegel by the very nature of modern arms, which no longer require man-to-man combat.

52. Hegel, *Natural Right,* 7: 372.

53. Such is the dialectic by which the individual generally rejoins the universal; finite life, being in itself negation of the negation, becomes identical to infinite life. Cf. our analysis on this dialectic of life and a living person in "Vie et prise de conscience de la vie dans la philosophie hégélienne d'Iéna," *Revue de métaphysique et de morale,* 1937.

54. Hegel, *Phénoménologie,* 2: 23.

55. Cf. Hegel's *Study of the German State,* in *Works,* ed. Lasson, 7: 3, which begins with "Germany is no longer a State." This study is, from the historical point of view, one of the most penetrating studies that Hegel has devoted to the problems of his time.

56. Hegel, *Natural Right,* 7: 372.

57. Cf. on this heroic conception of freedom the celebrated dialectic of "combat for life and death" in the *Phénoménologie,* 1: 158, a dialectic that is followed by the dialectic of the relations of master and slave, 1: 161.

58. Hegel, *Natural Right,* allusion to what is called the science of political economy, 373, the texts cited are likewise found on 373. In its entirety the *economic* ought to be subordinated to the *political.* Similarly legislation cannot be stated exactly by an abstract understanding. There is also some of the irrational, and the rational is only "that there is a decision."

59. On this role of war, causing national communities to disappear into an empire, cf. Hegel, *Phénoménologie* 2: 42–43.

60. Emile Bréhier, "Hegel," in *Histoire de la philosophie moderne* (Paris: Presses Universitaires de France, 1942), 773–74.

61. In the article on natural right in the *System der Sittlichkeit* (this system corresponding to the actual classes of German powers of the eighteenth century), Hegel, in the courses of 1805–1806, takes account of the profound changes in the social structure recorded by Napoleon's genius. The role of civil servants, having a sense of obligation and capable of preparing and enlightening public opinion, will become preponderant. In many respects Hegel is opposed to the liberal bourgeoisie whose development he reports. He places above it either a military aristocracy or an elite of civil servants capable of thinking through the substance of the State.

62. At the time of the *Phenomenology* in 1807, the great problem for Hegel appears to be the possibility of this rise of every individual to this awareness of the Universal. But such an elevation seems impossible to him in the State. The check of the revolution affects this point.

63. *Phénoménologie*, 2: 132. Hegel says again: "Therefore in this absolute freedom all the classes (*Stände*) are destroyed that are the spiritual essences in which the whole was articulated. The single consciousness, which belonged to such a member of this articulation, and which willed and performed in the midst of this particular member, abolished these barriers. Its goal is the universal goal, its language universal law, its work universal work."

64. Hegel, *Natural Right*, 7: 408.

65. Ibid., 409.

66. Ibid., 388. Cf. all the development on tragedy and comedy in the ethical life, 384–89.

67. That is why the development of comedy always accompanies the development of individualism. Ancient comedy is the sign of the decline of the city. Modern comedy, which is moreover so different, is a bourgeois comedy. Cf. on this point, Hegel, *Natural Right*, 7: 385–87.

68. "Such is the tragedy which the absolute eternally plays with itself. It is born in objectivity, gives in to its passion and death, and rises up from its ashes to grandeur."

Chapter V

1. On the evolution of Hegel's political thought we could consult Rosenzweig, *Hegel und der Staat*. On this political thought itself, such as it is found presented in the *Philosophy of Right* of 1821, cf. the Latin thesis of Jean Jaurès, *De primis socialismi Germanici lineamintis*, published as *Les Origines du socialisme allemand*, trans. Adrien Veber (Paris: Les Ecrivains Réunis, 1927). Jaurès reviews therein Luther, Kant and Fichte, Hegel and Marx.

2. Hegel, *Philosophie du droit* (Philosophy of Right), in *Works*, ed. Lasson, addition to paragraph 324, 6: 369.

3. The Hegelian state as it is presented in the *Philosophy of Right* is the product of historical evolution, but the knowledge that the philosopher grasps of it would not go beyond history absolutely. "To conceive what is, is the task

of philosophy, for what is, is reason. What concerns each individual is the child of its time; so also philosophy: *it sums up its time in thought.* It is as absurd to imagine that a commonplace philosophy will go beyond the contemporary world, as to believe that an individual will leap over his time, or will jump over Rhodes."

4. A large part of the *Phenomenology* is devoted to this problem, cf. the chapter on pleasure and destiny, the law of the heart and the delirium of self-conceit, virtue and the course of the world, etc.; Hegel, *Phénoménologie,* 1: 288 ff.

5. Hegel, *Phénoménologie,* 2: 129.

6. There was, however, an important political evolution of Hegel from 1805–1806 to 1821, but for what interests us here (the new notion of the State, civil society, the monarchy) our affirmation remains correct. The same is true concerning the appearance of absolute spirit different from objective spirit, which is found for the first time in the course of 1805–1806.

7. Hegel, *Realphilosophie,* 20: 251.

8. Hegel, *Realphilosophie,* 251.

9. Hegel, *Philosophie du droit,* Section 185, 156. In the ancient world the principle of particularity was the family, the Penates opposing the city. But in the modern world this principle has been deepened; it requires personal freedom, the choice of a profession, and so on. Plato's only *substantial* State is therefore no longer suitable. It is necessary, as Hegel says in the *Phenomenology,* that "substance also become *subject.*"

10. Hegel, *Realphilosophie* 1805–06, 20: 267. Morality, in the Kantian sense, is defined there as an elevation above the social state.

11. Hegel, *Realphilosophie,* 251.

12. Hegel, *Realphilosophie,* 251, note.

13. Hegel, *Realphilosophie,* 249.

14. Cf. already on this point the course of 1805–06, 20: 252.

15. Hegel, *Enzyklopädie,* para. 544, ed. Lasson, 5: 452.

16. *Realphilosophie,* 20: 245. "The universal will must be constituted starting with individual wills. But this "starting with" is only an appearance, for the universal will is what is *first;* it is essence. The Whole is prior to the parts, and individuals must be formed in the Universal by denying themselves, or by alienating themselves."

17. *Bildung.* Hegel gives a very broad meaning to this word culture. He indicates, moreover, the political formation of the individual as well as his economic formation, in general, his elevation to the Universal.

18. Hegel, *Realphilosophie,* 20: 246.

19. Ibid., 246.

20. "The power of the State that knows itself ought to have the courage to behave tyrannically in the case of necessity when the existence of the Whole is compromised." Hegel, *Realphilosophie* 20: 247.

21. Ibid., 247.

22. Ibid., 247–48.

23. There is, therefore, a destiny of great men of history comparable to that of the tragic heroes; they are representatives of a people or an era. But with their work accomplished, they ought to disappear. It is not the search for happiness that has driven them to power, but their "pathos." They ought to realize it, even in losing themselves.

24. The term "civil or bourgeois society" only appears furthermore in the *Philosophy of Right*.

25. And of "liberalism" and nothing more.

26. It is this definition of the State, starting with civil society, that Hegel really combats.

27. Hegel, *Philosophy of Right*, Section 258, 6: 195–96. Hegel adds what sums up exactly the purpose he intends: "Rationality consists in the intimate unity of the *Universal* and the *individual* . . . with regard to content in the unity of *objective freedom*, that is, of the general substantial will and of *subjective freedom* as individual consciousness and will, investigating their particular ends. . . ."

28. The description that Hegel gives in 1805 of the economic world is astonishing for his time.

29. Hegel, *Philosophy of Right*, Section 186, 6: 156.

30. Ibid., Section 187, 6: 157.

31. Hegel, *Realphilosophie* 20: 231.

32. Ibid., 232.

33. Ibid., 232.

34. Ibid., 232–233.

35. Ibid., 232–233.

36. Ibid., 233. In the *Phenomenology*, in the title "Rent Consciousness," Hegel describes the revolt of the person who sees himself submissive to a thing, namely, to money. He is inspired by *Le Neveu de Rameau* of Diderot; Hegel, *Phénoménologie* 2: 77 ff.

37. Hegel, *Philosophy of Right*, Section 245, 6: 189. Civil society is therefore driven (dialectically) outside itself. "This extention of relations offers also the means for colonization in which, in a systematic or sporadic form, a mature civil society is driven," 190–91.

38. Besides the family, the corporation constitutes the second moral origin of the State, that which is implanted in civil society. "The sanctity of marriage and professional honor are two axes about which the inorganic matter of civil society turns," Hegel, *Philosophy of Right*, 6: 193–94.

39. Hegel, *Philosophy of Right*, 6: 195.

40. Ibid., 169.

41. Ibid., Section 260, 202. As we see it, the synthesis Hegel intends is that of *substance* (general nonreflective will in itself) and *subject* ("subjectivity"). In the *Phenomenology* he has defined his philosophy as follows: "*substance* is moreover *subject*."

42. On this opposition, cf. the particularly interesting analysis of Hegel, *Philosophy of Right* Section 270, 207 ff.

Index